Traumatic Brain Injury

The Long Road Back

HOPE MOFFETT

To my husband Bill
who generously allowed this
story to be told, however painful
it was to remember, or
often to not remember.

Ring the bells that still can ring
Forget your perfect offering
There's a crack in everything
That's how the light gets in.

Leonard Cohen
From his song, *Anthem* ·

Bill and Hope with most of the grandchildren.

Foreword

Thoroughly unprepared we take the step into the afternoon of life.
Worse still, we take this step with the false presumption that our
truths and ideals will serve us as hitherto. But we cannot live the af-
ternoon of life according to the program of life's morning—for what
was great in the morning will be little at evening, and what in the
morning was true, will at evening become a lie.
　　　　C. G. Jung, Modern Man in Search of a Soul

Human beings are challenged to grow into what it means to be truly human and truly alive over the course of our lives. At certain pivotal points in life we have to let go of a familiar way of understanding who we are in order to acquire a new psychological identity that challenges us to incorporate new aspects of the self that long to be lived out in us. Gradual life drift makes these passages appear normal. But refusal to "grow up" leads to inevitable tensions and dramatic mid-life crises. But what happens when seemingly solid growth and development patterns are interrupted by a sudden and tragic event like a traumatic brain injury? How does one comprehend and understand what has occurred when that experience is so distant from one's history and sense of self?

This is what makes Hope Moffett's odyssey so brilliant. In his struggle back to health Bill Moffett is joined and accompanied by his wife, the author capturing this epic journey. Each endures his/her own travails, struggles with their own demons. Through dozens of vicissitudes each seeks to discover the revised goal of his/her life and the specific tools necessary to keep the faith in achieving the goals. Bill had Hope available and capable; but Hope struggled to find the emotional support each of us needs and expects from a pledged partner. Hope embraced her role most days, but the grueling sandpapering created by her new, but self-chosen career move—to focus her life energy on caring for Bill—strikes the reader. This period of psychological purification, fruitful waiting, and inner preparation for what life had in store for her is stimulating reading and profound modeling for psychological maturity.

Bill's sudden fall from personal, professional, and community glory without any deliberate self-injury or public act of embarrassment creates a Job-like call: "Why me, Lord?" To feel his limited return to health and the poverty of his current growth had to create daily pain. We feel it through Hope's portrayal of this mountain of a man devastated by a single unfortunate motor vehicle accident.

Like a voyeur we watch Bill and Hope painfully plow through times of struggle and experiences of consolation in their attempt to regain the stability and security they had achieved and believed they'd always have. Any reader can feel the pain, but wants to cheer the return to health of the entire Merletti and Moffett families. A challenging, but growth-producing read, especially for anyone struggling with a family member who undergoes a TBI.

Dennis Boike PhD
Family and Marriage Counselor

It reads fast and has almost a novel quality. It is compelling, for sure, even if you don't have a family member/friend with TBI. Unfortunately, the story does not end with an orchestral swell of all's well that ends well. The challenge continues. And that is what most of us don't get, even now.

Well done, dear friend...

Raelene Shippee-Rice PhD, RN
Associate Professor Emerita
University of New Hampshire

About this Book

This book began as a journal I wrote for—and to—Bill after our car accident on December 27, 2008 in Cape Coral, Florida. I wondered how he would otherwise make sense of what had happened to us when he awoke from his deep coma.

Little did I know then that there would be a long period of time after he awoke from the coma that he would also not remember. In the movies patients suddenly awaken one day and—shazam—they are back to normal. Like many Hollywood portrayals, this is not reality. Recovering from a coma is often a gradual process: one day being able to raise one finger when asked by the nurse to do so, then recognizing a family member before falling back into a deep sleep. The return to consciousness can take weeks.

Dealing with traumatic brain injury is different from any other injury. It is shocking to discover your loved one has turned into another person, often a person who not only does not recognize your efforts to care for him, but is belligerent. Broken bones don't create new personalities, but brain injury often does. I wondered if the changes in Bill's personality would last forever or would they recede as he recovered. Many nights my prayers were, "Please, God, bring him back." I didn't know how I would live with this person who looked like my beloved husband but often lashed out in hatred, someone whose demeanor I barely recognized.

To add to the dilemma, recovery is hard to trace in brain injury. It is uneven. It is a labyrinth of twists and turns that make each day a new challenge. There will be a day of surprising clarity, followed by one of blurred reality and depression. But if the changes are confounding to a loved one, imagine how disturbing it must be for the brain injured himself, to discover that simple things make no sense anymore.

For months, Bill could not understand a calendar. He'd gaze down at the page, shaking his head in confusion, shrug and say, "I just don't get it. Can you explain to me how you just know that today is Saturday?"

The emotional beating the caretaker of a brain-injured person often endures can be devastating. Especially if you are a loved one. That is why Doctor Gallagher, founder of Communicare rehab facility, told Bill that the injured person is not the only victim. "You tried to kick her ass out of here two weeks ago," he said. "You told her you wanted a divorce."

Bill said, "I did!? Boy I'm glad she didn't take me up on that!" He had no memory of that day.

So much about brain injury is unexpected. It creeps up on you and suddenly your own reality is challenged. Like when the need to get a financial guardianship arose. He had suddenly begun to talk about "managing" our finances. "I think I'm ready to buy and sell a few stocks," he said with new bravado.

It infuriated him that I would suggest that I control our finances. Even when Doctor Horn at Communicare, explained that it would be a temporary measure because his judgment was not yet up to par, he wasn't convinced.

He said, "If I have to have my spending monitored, then she needs to be monitored, too. She needs to get my signature to spend any money. What if she decides she's in love with the lawyer and they run off together?" I wanted to weep.

But hard decisions were not always limited to the facts of a brain injury. Who knew that Medicare would suddenly decide that it was time for Bill to vacate the facility where he was receiving care? That happens to patients with any kind of injury. When I asked the staff why we were being forced to move him to another level of care, the answer was, "We don't know. Medicare won't share their criteria with us, I guess for fear we will learn how to manipulate it. We just have to go along with it."

During the long months of Bill's recovery, several books were incredibly helpful. Lee and Bob Woodruff's *In a Second* made us feel that we were not alone. *A Stroke of Insight* by Jill Bolte Taylor affected Bill very much. We listened to tapes by Doctor Daniel Amen and spent hours watching his YouTube presentations.

It is our hope that our story will help other families facing brain injury—or any injury or illness that necessitates long hospital and rehab time.

Early January 2009

I'm sitting here tonight at my little desk in the kitchen, in our new home in Cape Coral, Florida. It is usually full of light, but tonight the single gooseneck lamp illuminates my desk, making it seem an island in the darkness. I know that if I don't write down what has happened to our life, it will get lost. And maybe it should. Perhaps we'll wish we could leave it behind us forever. But it is what we've been handed, and what we have to deal with now. It is our new reality.

I've written something for you each day. If you choose not to read it later, I'll understand. But, I've never felt so alone and writing to you forms a bond I can't experience in any other way right now as you lie in a coma in intensive care.

December 27, 2008

It happened so fast.

It was a splendid day here in the Cape, but then we have been finding since we bought this home, most days are. After a leisurely breakfast on the lanai, featuring fresh squeezed orange juice from fruit we had just picked from our own trees, we played in the pool, scrubbing away algae along the blue tiled water line. For years we had dreamed about having a vacation place in Florida to give us a break from New York winters. Now that we had retired, we were free to find a new life. Choosing this location had been easy. We had family here and good friends. Even though we'd only owned this house for a few months, it already felt like home.

You might think that we would have had a premonition, a sudden chill we recalled later, but there was none. There was no sign this would be our last day together in this carefree way, enjoying our new retirement.

It was your suggestion. "Shall we call John and Fran and see if they want to go out to dinner at the new restaurant Geo? Remember the place where we stopped on our way south, in Sarasota, that we liked so much? The same people own this restaurant."

"Sure," I said. "I'll bet John and Fran will be glad to go out and not have to cook. They've probably spent hours provisioning for their sailboat cruise tomorrow morning. I'm sure they're exhausted." I climbed out of the pool and walked through the sliding glass door to the phone on my desk in the living room, walking carefully so as not to slip on the white tile floor.

My three brothers and sisters-in-law and we had always stayed close emotionally, but had never lived close enough to one another that we could pick up the phone and have dinner together. John, the oldest of my three brothers, at 80, was still teaching student teachers and sailing. Our new winter home was only blocks away from him, his wife, Fran, and her son Chris. Years ago, John and Fran had taught us to sail, a hobby we had enjoyed every summer since. This close proximity felt special.

As I had suspected they were delighted by the dinner plan. John offered to drive and said they'd be by to pick us up at seven. They arrived in their van exactly on time and we climbed into the back seat, you on the passenger side and me behind John.

It was a gentle Florida evening and we were comfortable small talking as brothers and sisters do. We turned off Veterans Parkway onto Skyline Drive. (I wonder if you'll remember any of this.) John's cell phone rang.

Fran answered. "Your daughter wants to know if you will have breakfast with her tomorrow," she said to John, holding the phone up so he could respond. We approached the stop sign at the corner of Skyline Drive and Pine Island Road.

Still holding up the phone, Fran said, "I think you should turn left here."

It is not clear whether you were wearing your seat belt and threw it off, or whether you never had it on. You leaned forward over the console and yelled, "No, John, don't turn left. You go straight ahead here."

I wish we had known just how dangerous that intersection was. There was only a stop sign where there should have been a traffic light. Pine Island Road has four lanes with a median in the center. The speed limit is fifty-five miles per hour.

John saw a car coming from our left. He decided he could make it to the median safely. What he didn't see until he pulled out was the Rav4 SUV passing that car. I remember the sense of accelerating suddenly and Fran yelling, "John!"

Oh, somebody just got hit hard! It was a colossal crash. I thought it was happening on the other side of the highway.

When I opened my eyes, you were splayed over the console, not moving, your head at an awkward angle against the dashboard. I tried to touch you, but I couldn't reach. They told me later that we had been hit just behind where I sat, bending the frame of the car so badly that it lifted the end of my seat belt, suspending me. I remember thinking, as if in a dream, "This is bad. Something terrible has just happened to us."

When I awoke again, you were no longer in the car. I could see Fran through the passenger side window looking at the ground. Then two young men were lifting John from the driver's seat. "Oh my God, I'm so sorry," I heard him say.

Then a young man's face was close to mine. "We're going to get you out of here. We don't want you to strain at all. Just hug yourself and let us do all the work." I don't know how they got me unhooked from the seat belt, with my full weight on it and across the entire seat. The next I knew I was strapped to a board lying on the ground.

Bright lights were flashing. Sirens were screaming, getting closer. I could feel the vibration of footfalls near my head.

"Where is my husband?" I asked every time I felt someone coming near. Finally one of the EMTs, a young fellow with a sweet face, said, "Ma'am, we are taking care of you—and just you. We don't know about anyone else, but your husband is being taken care of by another team. We do know that."

"We've got to get out of here," I heard a man yell. "The helicopter is on the way and it needs space to land."

"Who is being airlifted?" I shouted, hoping someone would hear me.

A young man's voice answered. "Probably some of the people in the other car. We don't know for sure."

Still strapped to the board, I was lifted and slid into an ambulance. (Like a pizza into the oven, I remember thinking.) Suddenly a young woman appeared. Her face was close to mine in the dark interior, blocking out all other reality, as she asked question after question. I tried hard to answer correctly, feeling like a schoolgirl taking a test. I thought, with strange pride, "I must be okay if I can remember my social security number."

At the hospital, still strapped down, I was pulled from the ambulance and placed on a gurney with wheels. The EMTs, one on either side, ran with me down the hall. "How did you manage to arrange for a private room?" one of them joked. And then there were Michelle and Joe. She'd been at a Christmas party, on the phone waiting for her dad's response to her invitation to breakfast when she heard the crash and she could do nothing but wait. She said that finally Fran's son Chris had called her.

I had heard someone at the site saying that John wasn't being sent here to Lee Memorial so I said to Michelle, "Oh, Honey, your dad is at Cape Coral Hospital."

"That's okay, Auntie Hope," she said. "We're here for you and Uncle Bill. Chris and Fran are there with Dad." (Fran was the only one not injured.)

"Do you know where Bill is?" I asked her.

"They told us they're still working on stabilizing him."

A nurse leaned over me and said, "We want to take you over for a C-scan." I heard Velcro ripping away, as she gently tried to extricate me from the board. Then she attempted to help me sit up so she could take my shirt off.

But trying to bend shot pains everywhere, especially in my neck and back.

"I'm afraid we're going to have to cut your pretty shirt off," she said. But then, by working gingerly, she and another nurse got one arm out, then the other.

The circle of steel moved over my head. I closed my eyes.

4

Inside that dim space, the feeling that something must be terribly wrong with you loomed. I thought, surely someone would have had news if you were okay. I spent the entire seven minutes in the scan machine thinking, "Fight, Bill! Fight, Bill!"

I was back out in the brightly-lit hallway on a gurney when I saw, through a glass pane, my brother Art and sister-in-law Diana, rushing toward us. I wondered how they could have made it from Brandon so fast. And I wondered why they were here. But once they reached me they seemed calm and I thought, "This can't be too bad, or they would look more stressed. Maybe everything will be all right."

Then Michelle leaned over me and said, "Auntie Hope, a nurse is coming over from Uncle Bill's room."

Suddenly the nurse's face, ruddy and glistening with perspiration, was so close I could feel her breath. Her hair was drawn tightly back. "Your husband has been seriously injured," she said. "He has two broken vertebrae and several broken ribs, but what we're most worried about is his head injury. There may be brain stem damage."

"Brain stem? As in Christopher Reeve?" I asked.

"We won't know for a while. Just keep thinking positive thoughts." She patted my hand with a sad smile.

This seemed to happen in another world. Couldn't we just go home and finish cleaning the pool? The thought you might be quadriplegic was so foreign that it wouldn't settle in my brain. I heard the words, but their meaning escaped, as if the nurse had been talking in a foreign language.

"Meanwhile," she said, "we think it would be good if you could see him—speak to him. It is possible that he could hear your voice."

Of course! It was what I wanted to do.

She told the nurse taking care of me that they must get me in a wheelchair so I could fit into the small room where you were being treated. Gingerly, both nurses tried to lift my head to help me sit up, but the pain was so great, I passed out.

I came to in a few seconds. "Just give me a minute and try again."

As they tried to lift me, I could hear Art from what sounded like down a long tunnel. "Her eyes are rolling back again. I don't think this is going to work!"

I couldn't figure out why I hurt so much. Later one of the nurses told me that, ironically, I suffered from seat belt injuries. I had been thrown against the seat belt with great force, injuring muscles. When I looked at my body later I was amazed to see I was bruised black from my neck down to my groin.

I don't remember being taken to a room. I guess they gave me something to get to sleep, but every time I closed my eyes I heard the crash and my eyes popped open. I finally dozed off.

Sunday, December 28

Art and Diana were back at 6:00 in the morning. Art was determined he would be there when doctors did rounds in the intensive care unit where you had been transferred. Allen, who had been spending a few days over the Christmas holiday with his parents, was with them. Di and Allen stayed with me.

The nurse suggested that I try to take a walk, and although I still hurt everywhere, with Di's help I got out of bed. Walking wasn't so bad. When I got back in bed, I asked for a drink of water. I had just taken a sip when I retched, then passed out. Allen is close to being awarded his RN. He said he thought it was the vagus nerve causing the problem, that after serious injury this nerve is often affected, causing the exact symptoms I was suffering, retching and passing out. I was beginning to be aware of the nightmare we were facing. I knew that our life had changed, but I couldn't fathom how profoundly.

"Who was driving the other car?" I asked Art.

"All we know," he said, "is that it was a pregnant woman. Apparently she wasn't badly injured because they didn't even keep her overnight in the hospital. That's all we know now. Let's check with the insurance company before we try to contact her."

At about 10:00 a.m. our dear friends John and Jeanne Kremer arrived. I was so glad to see them. I asked if they would go see you and come back and report their impression.

In half an hour, they came back down to my room. John said, "Bill is in bad shape. There's no getting around that. But you know Bill. He's tough and I think he'll get through this."

John had a golf date that afternoon. He told me later that he played a few holes, then couldn't go on. He said all he could think about was you lying there with tubes everywhere. "I wondered what life would be like for our friends," he said, "if indeed Bill even made it. I thought there was a good chance, judging from the way he looked, that he wouldn't't."

Monday, December 29

Some of our kids, Andra, Kathy and Allison with two-month-old Jude, who she couldn't leave home because she was nursing, arrived today. I hadn't been able to see you yet because I'd been fainting, and probably because they wanted me a little more stable.

Andra wheeled me up to your room in the afternoon. I can't describe what a shock it was. You were hardly recognizable. Tubes ran from everywhere, one distending your mouth, pulling it downward. You were terribly swollen. Your left ear was filled with blood and your left eye bruised. Your neck was encased in a brace. I tried to talk to you, to tell you how much we love you and how we are going to tough this out like we have so many other things, but you were far away someplace. There was no response. I couldn't believe what I was seeing. How did this happen so quickly? Can't we just go back two days? Please, God?

I noticed that you were wearing your wedding ring. I asked the nurse in the room if it could be removed. With the swelling I was afraid it would cut off your circulation.

Using a lubricant, they were able to slip it off.

Andra had described your injuries from the charts she had read when she got in touch with family and friends after she first arrived: severe head trauma (right frontal bleed sub arch, left parietal region, left temporal bleed)—c7 facet fracture—left T1 Transverse process fracture—broken ribs 4-7.

In layman's terms you have a broken neck and cracked ribs, but it is the head injury that is so devastating.

Out in the hallway, I sobbed. "We had finally retired and we were doing so well, having such a good life. I thought we were the luckiest people in the world."

"I know. I know," Andra said, holding me and somehow keeping her own control, daughter comforting stepmother.

Tuesday, December 30

Today I was discharged. It is good being home with the kids. I still hurt everywhere, but I'd stopped passing out.

Your absence seems strange. I have gathered the newspapers and started a pile to save so that when you come home, you can catch up on the news. I imagine you out on the lanai with a glass of fresh juice, learning all that had happened while you were hospitalized. It gives me a vision I can hang on to.

Diana bought several steno notebooks for me so I can keep a journal. Obama's inauguration will be in two weeks. You will probably still be in the hospital, but I try to imagine us watching it together.

Wednesday, December 31, 2008

The kids and I decided this morning to surround you with only strength and positive messages. We took turns talking to you about how strong your body is and how impressed we are with your spirit. We know you will make it! We agreed that if we needed to cry we would take it to the waiting room where we'd have what Andra called a pity party.

In Intensive Care, the nurses' station is in the middle, with the rooms in a circle around it. In each room is a tragic story. As we talk to some of the loved ones of other patients, we hear their tales. A young woman, her arm protectively around her mother's shoulders, told us how her father, a farmer, had been moving his tractor from one field to another. He had been on the road just briefly when he was hit from behind, throwing his body thirty feet in the air and colliding with a telephone pole before being catapulted to the ground.

A mother told us about her young son who discovered his wife in bed with his stepbrother. He tried to slit his own throat. Only his mother's quick actions saved him, though it was a bloody cab ride to the hospital.

It seems strange that now we are one of the tragedies. "My parents were on their way out to dinner . . ." I heard Kathy telling folks in the waiting room.

I wonder if you will remember attending Christmas Day brunch at John and Fran's and talking for a long time with Lori, their friend who is a registered nurse. She told me about how careful she is when she goes home after a shift. She strips off all of her clothes and places them directly into the washer, then showers, before she touches anyone else. She said that many germs in the hospital have become resistant to antibiotics and therefore can be deadly. I remembered that talk and I have been super careful that anyone who goes near you washes their hands first. Amazingly, some workers forget. A therapist today dropped her glove on the floor, then tried to put it back on. I told her she had to start all over, washing up and getting new gloves. She looked sheepish as she peeled off the gloves.

Lori came in earlier today. She stood at the foot of your bed and said to the nurse attending to you, "Listen, I want you to understand something about this man. He may be chronologically 70 years old, but think of him as more like 40. He is a very strong, very intelligent man. He and his wife ran a trade magazine for the wine and grape industry for many years. They have just retired. Don't give up on him just because you think he is old."

The nurse stiffened. "We're not in the habit of giving up on patients."

"I know," said Lori, "but I know how it sometimes works, too."

Each day one of the neurologists makes rounds to see patients. Surrounded by the team responsible for patients' care: respiratory specialists, nurses and physical therapists, he usually goes from room to room. We are afraid to leave the floor even to go to the cafeteria for fear we will miss this important time to ask our many questions.

Today, he was seated at the nurses' station, surrounded by the team, as the patients' families came to him. When our turn came, I asked him, "Is there anything you can tell us . . . about what to expect . . . anything at all? Like . . . how long Bill's recuperation will take?" I was fighting tears.

"Nope," he said, crooking his thumb over his shoulder in the direction of your room, "Maybe that's all we get. With brain injury you never know."

I felt a sudden wave of anger, and it shot me full of strength. "Let me tell you something, Doctor. This is NOT all we get. What we are going to get is full recovery. Please do not enter my husband's room with what you have just said on your mind. We are not allowing any negativism in that room."

To my surprise, a smile crept over his face. "Okay," he said. "I'm all for that."

Tim has arrived, so now four of our kids, and Jude, are here. We have been taking turns, two of us staying with you while the others gather in the waiting room or run to the cafeteria for a cup of coffee. All of us have been reading everything we can get our hands on concerning traumatic brain injury (TBI) as well as going on line. Each called their own kids to tell them to draw pictures for the walls in Grandpa's room.

We are a blended family, each having brought three children to the marriage. Kathy, Mark and Rob are my biological children. Andra, Tim and Allison are Bill's. But after thirty years they're all our kids. We are blessed with nine grandchildren.

About 5:00 p.m. we left the hospital and stopped at John and Fran's on the way home. John was sitting at the dining-room table, head held straight up by the brace on his neck, which had been broken in the accident. He said the brace made him feel constantly claustrophobic.

Tim, standing across the table, said, "We want you to know, John, that we do not blame you for this accident. Any of us could have been driving."

John looked as if he might cry. "You'll never know how much that means to me," he said. "I have had nightmares that you kids would blame me."

Their front door was open; fireworks appeared over neighbors' rooftops. That's when it dawned on me—this was New Year's Eve. I suddenly wanted to get out of there. We would not be celebrating. I was already on edge and the fireworks were making me think of people getting hurt.

We stopped at the Mexican restaurant on Del Prado Boulevard and bought our takeout dinner there.

At home, we piled the packages on the dining room table, opened a bottle of wine and made lots of toasts to your recovery.

Tim proved once again that he sure inherited your wacky sense of humor. Halfway through dinner, he said, "I know that Dad doesn't know the difference if we're there or not, but I have this guilty feeling we should be there with him."

Nobody answered.

"Maybe we should go out and buy a pointy hat and go to the hospital. We could dress him up with the hat and some streamers and take some pictures, so he'll know later . . ."

We all burst into hysterical laughter—that for most of us turned quickly to sobs.

Everyone was in bed by about ten, exhausted and wanting to be rested for the days ahead.

New Year's Eve seemed so inconsequential.

Thursday, Jan 1, 2009

You have been in ICU for four days. One of the articles Tim read said music sometimes gets through to an injured brain so he went to Walmart and bought a CD player that we keep running constantly, playing all your favorites, everything from Jimmy Buffet to Vivaldi and Mozart.

None of us have seen TV or read a paper. Our total focus has been narrowed to you and one another. I am trying hard to avoid hysteria or panic. It may take a long time, but you WILL get better, and we will have years of happiness ahead. I say it over and over, but still this new reality still seems strange.

The kids have been fantastic. I am so proud of them. The accident seems to have proved to them how much they love you. They are supporting you—and me—in every way.

Friday, January 2

The phone rang at 3:20 this morning, scaring the wits out of me. "Oh, no, please," I prayed. "No bad news." But it was the ICU nurse asking permission to install a direct line to your largest vein. It has been difficult to draw blood because your body is so swollen. This will make that easier and also possible to monitor your fluids. I gave permission, hoping it was the right decision, then had a hard time falling back to sleep.

We drove to the hospital in two cars this morning, but could not see you because they had not completed installing the line to your vein. Kathy, Andra and I went back to the house to fix lunch for everybody (leftover Mexican) but Tim, Allison and Jude stayed a while longer. When they arrived home, they were ecstatic. They had gotten in to see you, and when Nurse Jenny asked you to hold up two fingers, you did!

Matthew just called. You know how twelve year olds hate to talk on the phone, but he wanted a complete report on how Grandpa was doing. When Kathy told him about your holding up two fingers, he yelled, "Cool!"

Nurse Cathy, who has been very kind to us, came into your room this afternoon. She wanted to explain to us what had happened and what she thought would be your prognosis. Everyone else has been telling us, "No way of knowing with a brain injury," so we were eager to hear what she had to say.

She explained that memories are laid down in the brain in layers, with the most recent closest to the surface. Thus, when traumatic brain injury occurs, the amount of memory lost depends on the depth and severity of the injury. She said that when patients are just coming back to consciousness, because memories of childhood are buried deep in the brain, they often act childlike, even sometimes talking baby talk. This could be simply a stage until healing begins and memories begin to work their way up through the layers.

We asked her what she thought of your potential for recovery.

"Excellent," she said. "He has a lot going for him. Obviously, he is a strong man, physically and mentally—and he is a fighter. It is clear that he has tremendous family support and that is a very important factor. I think this guy's coming all the way back. But, remember, brain injuries take time to heal. Give him 18 months."

She stayed with us about 45 minutes and by the time she left we all felt such relief. Eighteen months? We can do that! At last, some hope that our lives will return to normal.

We are living in a strange world. We know you are badly hurt, but we do not understand, really, what this will mean to our future.

It has been a long time since we have all been together, and now we're joined in one purpose. I feel guilty enjoying the kids' company so much.

Rob and Jen were scheduled to arrive from California this evening. The rest of us had dinner at Mel's Diner because it placed us closer to the airport. It was near 11:00 p.m. when their plane arrived.

Tomorrow Andra, Tim and Allison, with baby Jude, must fly directly to Minneapolis to attend their grandfather's funeral. He was their mother's father. He died on December 28, the day after our accident, at the age of 102. What a month this has been for the Moffett kids! When they packed to come here, they brought only summer clothes. Their mother will take winter clothes for them to Minneapolis. Just as they were about to leave, Andra picked up your maroon cashmere sweater and threw it over her shoulders. "I'm taking this," she said. "It'll keep me warm and make me feel closer to Dad."

Saturday, January 3

Today you had an inferior vena cava filter installed in the main artery leading up your leg. This was explained in this way: Imagine a small closed-mesh umbrella being inserted into the artery, then being opened. Blood can pass through, but it will protect you from having blood clots reach your lungs, and will probably stay there for the rest of your life.

Tonight, Kathy, Jennifer and I were keeping vigil in your room. Kathy and Jen were on either side of your bed, talking to you. Jen asked Kathy if you could open your eyes.

Kathy said, "Bill, you would make us all so happy if we could see your eyes open."

I don't know what made her say that because you have been unresponsive, but suddenly, we could see you struggling, and finally—with such great effort—you got them open! You stared straight ahead, not focusing, but obviously you'd heard Kathy.

We were stunned! We had to leave the room, all of us crying. We ran down to the waiting room to tell the others. You are in there!

The nurses assure us you will remember none of this, but when I see you grimace it breaks my heart. I can't imagine how much pain you must be in.

Tonight, just as we were leaving, a woman stopped me in the dimly-lit hallway. "Your daughter, Kathy, was very kind to me yesterday," she said. "You have a lovely family. I wanted to tell you that three years ago, a teen-aged, drunk driver struck me. I was thrown a long way and sustained severe brain injury. But I am here today, fully recovered. It takes a long time, but stay strong." What a wonderful message. I was so grateful to her for sharing this.

Mark cooked dinner tonight. He had arrived earlier in the week. Unfortunately, he had thrown his back out just before departing from Corning. It is uncomfortable for him to sit or stand around at the hospital, so today he decided to stay home and sit by the pool. When we arrived home it was wonderful to be greeted by a lovely dinner.

Sunday, January 4

A milestone: You opened your eyes spontaneously when we came in this morning! Even though they are still not focusing, we are encouraged.

You are suffering so much. Your body is building up lots of phlegm and you need to be suctioned regularly. That is so hard to watch. A tube is inserted into your throat and it must make you feel like you're choking and hurt like hell. The nurse says they won't have to do this as often once the tracheostomy is in.

Monday, January 5

Nurse Cathy called early this morning and said that they are installing your tracheostomy and so far it has gone well. "The procedure will take most of the morning," she said, "so there is no reason to hurry in."

Having a tracheotomy will allow them to remove the tube from your mouth. The trach tube will go through an incision in your throat directly into your windpipe. The nurses have told us it will make you much more comfortable. Here is an explanation I looked up online for how a tracheostomy is installed:

- *The patient is supine with head extension and under general anesthesia.*
- *Incision is 2–3 cm from the second tracheal ring down.*
- *Divide the thyroid isthmus if needed.*
- *Make a hole between the third and fourth tracheal rings, removing the anterior portion of tracheal ring.*
- *Tracheostomy tube is inserted.*

This sounds complicated. I will be happy when it is done and you have come through it without complications.

I am taking advantage of this time this morning to attack a high pile of bills and papers on my desk. I look out through the open sliding-glass doors to the pool in the lanai—so close that if you were here and jumped in now you would splash water into the living room. I realize that none of us have even thought about taking a dip.

This afternoon Respiratory Therapist John tried to wean you off the ventilator so the tracheostomy can work for you.

This was the hardest of anything so far to watch. You rasped and struggled and looked like you weren't getting enough oxygen.

John assured us this was normal. He was suctioning your throat and lungs regularly. The procedure looked very painful. When he said he would let you breathe on your own for two hours, I felt faint.

"Don't worry," he said. "We'll be watching him. We won't let him suffocate."

John is pleased with the results and plans to ask the doctor if you can be taken off the ventilator tomorrow.

I have been so nervous when I am in the room alone with you because it is hard to know when something is an emergency and when it isn't. Does that beeping mean something dangerous is happening? When should I call for help? What are the signs? What if I sat here not calling for help and you died?

Those fears were somewhat assuaged later this afternoon. When Rob came in your room and we all rushed to greet him, we didn't realize how loud we were talking.

A nurse rushed into the room. "What in heaven's name are you people doing?" he said. "The patient's blood pressure has shot sky high!"

We were embarrassed. We should have known better. But we learned that someone is constantly monitoring your vital signs. And—you are hearing and responding to outside stimuli.

Tonight, Rob and Jen stood by your bed to say goodbye. They must return to California tomorrow and are very sad.

Rob was holding your hand, and said, "I love you, Bill." He looked up with tears in his eyes and said, "He squeezed my hand, Mom!"

Jen leaned in close to your face. You know how you and she have always kidded. "We have to leave now," she said, "because you have talked our legs off!"

You laughed! Laughed! Then you raised her hand to your lips.

We were stunned.

As we reached the doorway, Rob and Jen turned and waved,

You waved back!

We stood in the hallway in a circle hug, crying partly out of ecstasy at your response and partly out of sadness that they must leave.

Tuesday, January 6

When I arrived this morning, Nurse Cathy told me that earlier you'd mouthed, "Where's Hope?"

Wow. This is hard to believe!

She came with me into your room and leaned in close to you. "Can you tell her how much you love her?"

You turned your head to look at me and mouthed the words, "I love you."

My knees buckled. Please, please continue to fight your way out.

During the day, it became harder and harder to watch you still sounding full of phlegm, struggling to get enough air. It was damned scary. Therapist John said you were doing well, but it sure didn't look like it.

Lori told me it is important that you get physical therapy immediately. I told her no one has even tried to sit you up. I asked the physician's assistant why.

He said, "Well, your husband is a big man, and to sit him up would take three people. We just don't have that kind of manpower. They're short-staffed in physical therapy."

I asked him to contact the head of that department. When he handed me the phone I asked the woman on the other end if she would come and meet with me. She arrived quickly.

"Look," I said, "my husband must have physical therapy. His life depends on it. I know you're short-staffed, but we're willing to hire someone. I just need your guidance on this."

"We're not short-staffed," she said. "We had an order to not go into your husband's room because of a cardiac issue."

It had been a miscommunication. That afternoon, three therapists arrived. I am seeing firsthand how important it is for a patient to have an advocate present every minute. You can't speak for yourself and a simple slipup like this could cost you your life.

What an ordeal it was to get you sitting up. Your back is stiff from having lain in bed so long and your broken ribs must be very painful.

Lori stopped by during your session. She told me to kneel in front of you. While she and the other therapists pushed from behind, she shouted to you, "Go to Hope, Bill. Try to reach Hope."

You tried so hard, your eyes full of pain.

It was awful.

20

Thursday, January 8

My brother Chas arrived from New York today. Before that I had been alone for a few days. I say alone, but I have never spent the night alone, thanks to John and Fran who have spent many nights with me, and John and Jeanne Kremer, who have done the same. Thank God for my brothers and friends.

When Chas and I got in this morning, we were surprised to see you sitting in a wheelchair. It is called a cardiac chair and it allows the staff to transfer you lying down to the chair, which then is cranked up to a sitting position.

The last time Chas saw you, you were the picture of health, and I could see the shock on his face, but he quickly covered it. "Hi Bill. It's Chas. How're you doing?"

You gazed off into space. If you were in there this morning, we couldn't see it.

We sat near you, I in the chair and Chas on the edge of the bed. Chas continued his one-way conversation. "It's really good seeing you sitting up. I didn't know what to expect, but this is really encouraging . . ."

When you were returned to bed, you were exhausted. You had lots of phlegm and were coughing. Judging from your grimaces, you hurt. Chas and I spent the day taking turns keeping a cool cloth on your forehead and that seemed to make you more comfortable.

Another surprise at rounds today. Doctor Dru said he thinks you are ready to be transferred to neuro stepdown, an eight-bed unit, the next step after intensive care.

I don't know whether to be happy or sad. In intensive care, I know you are getting round-the-clock care. You still seem so fragile, so vulnerable. But Doctor Dru explained that he tries to get patients out of intensive care soon because the risk of infection is so great here.

A nurse from his entourage spoke up and said, "Sorry, Doctor, but there is a list of 15 patients waiting to be transferred to neuro stepdown." The doctor looked disappointed.

A few minutes later a nurse came into your room with pamphlets describing long term care facilities in the area.

I never dreamed you would have to leave the hospital and transfer to a nursing home. I imagined you staying here until you were well enough to come home. I feel like I'm in this never-never land, needing to make life changing decisions, without knowing the rules.

Out in the hall, Chas had engaged the doctor in a conversation concerning how medical training has changed over the years. I've never seen the doctor so relaxed. While they were still chatting, a nurse entered and said, "We have a bed in neuro stepdown."

Just like that. And in fifteen minutes we were following your gurney to the elevators.

Friday, January 9

When Chas and I arrived at your bedside this morning, we were shocked. Your hands had been tied down to your sides. You were straining against the restraints. We noticed you have developed eczema on your face that must itch and drive you crazy. Apparently that is why you had not been shaved.

We quickly untied your hands and vowed that we will stay with you every minute if need be. You have to be able to scratch your own face! I will NOT allow you to have your hands tied down. Maybe you won't remember this, but the effect of being tied down will live on in your brain.

Last night when we left, the nurse told us you would be bathed and shaved today. Neither has happened. We quickly realized that you had soiled the bed. It took half an hour to get a nurse to respond to our light. When she finally arrived, she said, "I just cleaned him at seven. He'll have to wait his turn." And she turned and left.

She returned in about fifteen minutes and apologized. "We are so short-staffed here. We just have to do our best. I'm sorry to have spoken so harshly to you."

Finally, a young CNA (Certified Nurse's Assistant) arrived and between us, we got you bathed. As she pulled your covers up around your shoulders, she noticed that your trach tube was crooked. She reached to fix it. I grabbed her hand. "You can't touch his trach after just cleaning him!"

She looked contrite. "I forgot," she said.

The hospital workers try so hard, and mostly, do a great job, but just one instance of introducing bacteria through this kind of mistake could be fatal. They work twelve hour shifts and by the end of the shift, they are exhausted. But this adds to my feeling that we must be constantly vigilant.

I realize that I can't leave you here alone at night. I spent the rest of the day on the phone hiring private duty nurses to spend the nights with you. The first arrived at 5:00 p.m. and appeared very competent. I told her I wanted you kept clean and comfortable and that you were not to have your hands tied down.

Tonight I left with Chas, feeling confident that you would have individual care and never have to wait for attention.

I had forgotten about tickets we had bought for Broadway Palm Dinner Theater before the accident until Jeanne Kremer called to remind me. Chas urged me to go. He said it would be good for me—and for Fran—to get away. He would spend the evening with John. Art and Diana also had tickets, as did John and Jeanne Kremer. We had seats together.

What a weird night. I felt on the verge of tears throughout dinner and the beginning of the show. "What in heaven's name am I doing here?" I thought. I felt lost and out of place. My world had become the hospital and home—anything else felt alien.

Then some of the music and lyrics of "Singin' in the Rain," seeped in and I actually found myself laughing!

It is amazing how a good laugh can refresh a weary body and soul.

Saturday, January 10

It's been two weeks. I noticed this morning that the stack of newspapers sitting next to my desk in the kitchen has reached about a foot high. I'm facing the fact that you will be hospitalized longer than I originally envisioned and my idea of saving the papers is probably not practical. But I immediately rejected the thought of throwing them out—as if it would be an admission that you might not return.

When we arrived at the hospital Lori was in your room, Even though you now have a private duty nurse, she had changed your bed, given you a bath and rubbed your back. She is such a wonderful nurse and friend. She'd had a private duty case on another floor, but came to see you before going home. She tried chatting with you, but you didn't respond.

"Darn," she said, "I really hoped we could get him into Lee Memorial rehab right here. They are so good, very aggressive and they do wonders with brain injuries, but I just don't think he's ready. He has to be able to work three hours a day."

Lori motioned for me to join her in the waiting room to talk about what the next step is likely to be, leaving Allison and baby Jude, who had returned, at your bedside. I worry about Jude spending so much time in this germ-infested hospital, but everyone is being very careful with him, not allowing him to touch anything, and always washing hands before picking him up.

Suddenly, Allison burst into the waiting room. "He's asking for you, Hope. He said so clearly, 'Where's Hope?'"

Lori and I rushed back to your room.

When I came up to your bed, you put your arm around me and looked right into my eyes. This was the first time you had focused—and it felt eerie in a way.

"Hey!" Lori said. "Maybe we CAN get him into rehab here."

~

We understand the rules a little better now, but the knowledge is not making us happy. Medicare decides how long patients may stay at any level of care. We are in a bind. Medicare has decided that you are ready to move out of neuro stepdown. The next step is rehabilitation. But if they can't accept you here at Lee Memorial, we may have to place you in a nursing home, euphemistically referred to as long term care.

This afternoon Chas and I went to look at two facilities in Cape Coral. The people there were friendly and the facility looked clean, but the halls were lined with pitiful folks in wheel chairs, many drooling.

When we returned to the car after visiting the last facility, Chas said, "What did you think?"

"I think if we put him in here he will either think he's bought the farm, or it will be his greatest motivation to get better. Unfortunately, I think the former. God, I don't want to do this to him."

Sunday, January 11

I awoke this morning at 5:00 a.m. and called the hospital. Your nurse said you had been restless all night, waving your right arm around as if it was numb or hurt. I went back to sleep and the next thing I knew it was 7:45. Nuts! I rushed into the living room where Chas was fully dressed, sitting in an armchair, reading a book.

"Damn!" I said. "I overslept."

"It's okay," Chas said. "Remember you added a nurse to the day shift so you can relax a little."

Still, I felt panicky and threw my clothes on in a hurry.

Good thing. At 8:00 a.m. Nurse Carol called from the hospital. "Your private duty came in this morning and she looks sick," she said. "She can't seem to hold her head up."

Chas and I were out the door in minutes.

When we arrived thank goodness Lori, who had again been working private duty nearby, was there, staying close to you so the sick-looking private duty caretaker couldn't breathe on you.

I signaled the poor young woman into the hallway and told her she needed to go home. Then I called the agency.

They were very contrite and sent a replacement who arrived in about an hour. But the bliss I felt at having backup has dissipated. You just can't let down your guard.

Here's something else: You haven't moved your left leg. Your left arm is still weaker than your right, but seems to be improving. Another truth to be faced. Your injury on the right side of your head could well have rendered your left leg useless. At an earlier time, this would have seemed catastrophic. Now, it seems like just one other issue to deal with. If we can get your brain okay, dealing with a useless left leg seems down the scale of importance.

The kids have all sent photos and they are pasted up all over your walls. There is a Thanksgiving family portrait with us surrounded by our six kids, five spouses and nine grandchildren. Whenever a new caretaker comes into the room, I guide them over to the wall of pictures before I allow them to approach your bed. "I would like you to meet Bill Moffett," I tell them, pointing to you in the picture. He is only temporarily that person over there. This is the person he is and will return to being. When you talk to him, please keep this picture in your mind."

This afternoon a smaller trach was installed. Apparently the procedure was hard on you. You must have an obstruction in your throat because it has always been difficult for you to be intubated. When you were returned to your room, you were coughing hard and that alone was making you miserable. Your eyes were big and seemed to plead for help. Finally a nurse gave you some morphine and you were able to settle down. Why this wasn't given to you before the procedure, I don't know.

We are still hoping to have you accepted into the rehabilitation program here at Lee Memorial, but you have "failed" two evaluations. This morning an evaluator, a thin, humorless woman, came to try once again, but emerged from your room after only a minute or two and said, "Sorry, we will not be able to admit him at this time. He is babbling in there."

I am feeling panicky. I do not want to put you in a long term care facility. I have put out a message on CaringBridge. This is a wonderful website that Andra and Tim set up for us during the first days after the accident. It allows caretakers to post how their loved ones are doing and others to pick it up as e-mail, saving the caretaker from having to send endless messages. I asked our friends and extended family to look in their areas for rehab facilities. I don't care where it is, if they accept you, we will work it out somehow.

You are still lying in bed all the time except when the physical therapy team is here. The swelling has abated but you are beginning to look haggard. Your hair hasn't been cut and is now getting longer than you have ever worn it.

It's clear that you want to communicate with us, but we can't understand what you are trying to say. It is very frustrating for us—and must be much worse for you.

When Chris came in this afternoon, he placed his ear right down next to your mouth. After a minute, he turned to me, "Could we talk out in the hall for a minute?"

In the hallway Chris said, "I heard him clearly. He said, 'What happened?' I don't know what to say to him."

"I'll talk to him."

I returned to your bedside and leaned over you. "We have been in an accident," I began.

You surprised me by pushing me away and motioning for Chris.

"You have been in a bad accident," Chris said, "but you're getting better."

You shook your head.

"Honestly," Chris said. "You are getting better, Bill."

You nodded then, just faintly, but seemed to relax.

I am so glad Chris thought of such a simple method—putting our ears next to your mouth—to help us communicate instead of trying to read your lips. Matter of fact, I feel stupid for not having thought of it.

After Chris left, you motioned for me to come close. This time I did put my ear right next to your mouth. Your voice was raspy but I could understand you. You said, "We have a situation here. We are going to have to learn . . ." You drifted off.

I can't imagine being inside your head right now. The confusion must be debilitating. And yet you understand that you are hurt. And, true to form, you are trying to control it.

Monday, January 12

Your voice gets stronger almost by the hour. But often what you are saying makes no sense.

I was alone with you for a little while this afternoon. You babbled on about cooking dinner. "Don't worry about it," you said. "Just remember to stir the wine very slowly into the sauce or it will curdle."

I guess I should be encouraged that you are remembering your gourmet cooking.

I was standing looking out the window, wondering what life will hold for us. I saw a couple about our age, walking hand in hand and suddenly my throat was swelling. Will we ever be a couple again? I tried not to let myself get low, but finally I couldn't hold back the sobs. I held my hand tightly over my mouth to cover the noise. You just kept rambling on . . .

As your recovery progresses you are becoming increasingly agitated. You pull at your trach and yank the blood oxygen monitor off your middle finger. It means one of us needs to be with you every moment. Thank God—again—for family.

I look around at some of the others in this unit and know how fortunate we are. If we had been younger when this happened, had small children, I could not have dedicated my life to taking care of you, as I have now. And we have an incredible family—and good friends. The difference of what happens to a patient with traumatic brain injury with and without this support can be enormous—life or death. A brain-injured patient is vulnerable, at the mercy of any caretaker. And no matter how well intentioned, these people get tired. They make mistakes. Just one of these mistakes can trigger events that become a slippery slope to death.

You have been refused admission to the rehab unit here at Lee Memorial, so we must find another place to which you may be transferred. Time is running out. The physician's assistant at the front desk, whom I have dubbed Quasimodo, tells me you will have to be transferred within days. Right now the only option is the nursing home. I wish we could wake up from this nightmare, but now I know it won't be a "movie" awakening, but a long, slow process.

Physical therapy technicians are coming regularly now and it is always difficult for you. Today as they were pushing and pulling, trying to get you sitting up, you looked at me and said, "Aren't you going to protect me from this pain?"

"Where do you hurt?" I asked.

"Just everywhere," you said.

In some ways it was easier when you were "out," not seeming to feel your pain.

During your waking hours, you are now talking nonstop. Most of it is cooking. "We're going to be just fine," you say. "This is a special party for our family who loves us. It has to be right. Diana, you get the fish. Art, you and Hope get the room set up. Don't panic." The old bossy Bill is emerging and this elates us. Your caretakers say this is great progress. You are working your way through your layers of memory.

A strange thing happens sometimes. Just as I'm falling asleep I think of something you have done that day and I think, "I have to call Bill and tell him about this."

Wednesday, January 14

The social worker knows how panicked I am about your next step because I have camped on her doorstep every day, as has Chas, even from long distance when he had to return to Long Island. Today she asked me to join her and the liaison from Lee Memorial Rehab in the waiting room for a meeting. "We have a proposition for you," she said. "You are going to have to move Bill out of the hospital environment, yet he is not ready for the rigors of rehab here. We propose that you move him to assisted living, and then maybe in a week or two he will be ready to be admitted to rehab here." Assisted living is another euphemism for nursing home.

I have a sinking feeling. What protection do we have? What if once you are out, they continue to say you're not ready to be admitted and you have to stay in assisted living? Maybe I'm being paranoid, I feel as if I have my back against the wall.

This afternoon, Peter Knott called. He had sent a long, detailed report of a rehab facility he had found in Sarasota, near his winter home in Bradenton. *Peter and Joette Knott are close friends with whom we share time both in Florida and in New York and are sailing buddies as well.*

You remember hearing them speak of their friend Jude LeBlanc, a retired radiologist from New York? Jude and his wife were visiting the Knotts, and Peter and Jude decided to forego a day of vacation to look at facilities for you as soon as they'd read the message I'd sent out on CaringBridge asking friends to look for facilities in their areas. They looked at several places, but Peter said that when they found HealthSouth they were elated. "It is bright and immaculate," Peter said. "And Jude was impressed with the opportunities—a small gym on the second floor and a much larger one on the first floor—that offer any equipment you could imagine for rehabbing people, especially those with brain damage."

I immediately called the social worker and asked her to contact HealthSouth to see if they would send someone out to evaluate you. This is another protocol that seems strange: To be transferred from here to a rehab unit, we need the hospital social worker to obtain the paperwork from the rehab facility.

Your acceptance there is a long shot and I know it. If you are not ready for rehab here, why would I think they will take you there? But we will not leave a stone unturned. And we will pray.

Thursday, January 15

When I arrived in the morning, the nurse on duty told me you had spiked a fever during the night. "Don't know what this is about," she said, "but we think we should keep him here at least another day just in case he is coming down with something." We pray that God has intervened to give us another day—and that you are not getting sick.

You were fidgety. "Get me out of here," you pleaded over and over.

Then suddenly you asked me, "You know what is interesting? How we communicate only you don't believe."

I leaned over you. "I do believe."

Becoming more agitated, you said, "What do you believe?"

"I believe that you are getting better and better."

Suddenly you threw your arm around my head. I wasn't sure what you would do. It scared me. I didn't have time to struggle as you pulled me down . . . and kissed me.

By late morning there was still no word on when they will kick us out of here or whether or not you will be accepted at HealthSouth. I called the Craig facility in Denver this morning. It is said to be the best in the country. I know I'm grasping at straws, but maybe one of them will be our answer. Craig's agent said that it would not make sense for us to fly you there so they could work with you for a few weeks and then fly you back here. It would be too disruptive, he said. "Try to find a facility closer to your home."

I am trying! I wanted to shout.

Next call was to HealthSouth. Yes, they had received your paperwork yesterday. Their liaison plans to be here this afternoon! Now I will really pray hard, because you are slated to be discharged tomorrow. Your fever is down, and according to Medicare, there is no reason to keep you here any longer.

Around 1:00 p.m. the liaison from HealthSouth, a full figured, vivacious redhead arrived. I brought her into your room and said, "Bill, this is Annette. She is here to evaluate you to see if you can be admitted to a facility named HealthSouth."

"Annette, I know that name," you said.

I explained to her that Annette is my middle name.

You reached up to her. "Get me out of here, will you?"

"I'll take him," she said. Just like that!

I was stunned.

Out in the hallway, she said, "We'll send an ambulance to pick him up tomorrow. Look, Sweetie, HealthSouth performs miracles. You're going to begin to see great changes now. They'll have him walking in three weeks." "Three weeks?!"

"Yep. His injury has created something like a snowstorm in his brain. You know those little balls that you turn upside down and all the snow-flakes come down? That's still happening in his brain. In a month, when all of this begins to settle down we'll know much more."

When I called Art and Diana and told them the news that you'd be moving to HealthSouth, they dropped everything—again—and were here within two hours.

Annette told us you will be dressed the first day you are there. "We don't want anyone in hospital gowns," she said. "We don't want them thinking of themselves as patients. Go out and get him some sweat pants and shirts. Get a couple of zip-up sweatshirts, and because of his neck brace, try to have all of his shirts with a wide neck. Label all of his clothes. The only thing to remember is that the availability of beds changes, sometimes by the hour. I think we will still have a bed for him tomorrow, but I'll get in touch with you in the morning."

So Art, Diana and I left the hospital about 5:00 p.m. and rushed to Target. We found most of what we needed there. We got home about seven and labeled everything, packing it into a suitcase. It suddenly dawned on me I would not be able to come home every night since Sarasota is over an hour away and I was surely not going to leave you there alone your first few nights, nor did I think I would be up to the drive after the long days I expected we would put in. So I threw a few things in a suitcase for myself. Around eight, we realized that we had not had dinner. We settled for peanut butter toast.

I am having a hard time falling asleep. Yesterday I was in despair, picturing you in a wheelchair in the hallway of the extended care facility. Tomorrow we will be in an entirely new place that sounds perfect. I am so grateful to Peter. Yet, knowing how to react is hard. I try to follow the advice of not getting too high on good days or too low on days that nothing seems to go right. But I'm holding in a "Whoopee!" And I'm sending a big hug to Peter!

Friday, January 16

Annette's call came about 8:00 a.m. "I have bad news and I have good news" she said.

I felt faint.

"The good news is we have a bed available. The bad news is that we can't get Medicare to pick up the transportation cost."

I let out the breath I'd been holding in. These days I have been telling myself, that somehow we'll pay for whatever is needed. Having to pay for an ambulance seemed like such a small issue.

We arrived at Lee Memorial at 9:00 a.m. The ambulance was scheduled to arrive at 10:00.

It did not arrive at 10:00, was still not there at 11:00.

We paced like expectant parents. I asked the nurse if I could ride in the ambulance with you. The nurse explained it was against the rules but that the drivers had agreed to let your nurse, Roz, accompany you. I'm so glad you won't be alone. Roz has been the best nurse we've had, always able to calm you down, always remaining very gentle.

Finally at noon, a crew of two men arrived and transferred you to the gurney that would take you to the ambulance. When I kissed you goodbye and told you we would see you again in a little over an hour, you look confused.

Our plan was to follow the ambulance in Art and Di's van. They insisted I sit in the front passenger seat for the trip to Sarasota. They had bought a sandwich and tea for my lunch. After I finished eating, Art said, "Why don't you recline the seat and try to rest until we get there. We've got an hour's ride ahead of us." I promptly fell into a deep sleep, snoring loudly, they told me later, and awakened only as we were pulling into HealthSouth's driveway.

We found the grounds pretty, nicely landscaped, with a small lake near the parking area. A receptionist in the lobby politely asked us to sign in. Attractive art hung on the walls that were painted in restful pastels. And just as Peter reported, everything appeared immaculate.

By the time we arrived on the second floor, you had been wheeled into your spacious, sunny room, and were in bed.

Two nurses were looking you over, head to toe. "We want to be sure there is no skin condition," one explained. They are treating you with kindness and respect and calling you "Mr. Moffett." At the hospital I had asked several CNAs not to talk baby talk to you, not to yell, and please not to call you "Honey" or "Sweetie."

A nurse entered the room and offered to give us a quick tour of the floor while your entrance exam was being completed. At one end was a small therapy room/gym. Beds were on either side of the room on which clients were being exercised by several physical therapists. At the ends of the room were stationary bikes and tables with pegboards and other "games" for patients.

The rooms were all large and airy. Several small meeting rooms were used for one-on-one speech and occupational therapy.

A fiftyish dark-haired man, good-looking, dressed in a white coat, approached us in the hallway and introduced himself as Doctor DeJesus. He said most people here called him Doctor D, but I like saying DeHaysus. He is the head of this facility and will be your main physician here. "Your husband will have a team of caretakers," he explained. "He will be seen regularly by a neurologist, an internist and a psychologist. At the beginning he will also see a psychiatrist, who may prescribe medications that might help him begin to focus his thoughts."

After our struggle to find a proper place for you, now seeing you receiving such excellent care made me feel almost giddy.

Back in your room, Doctor DeJesus leaned over your bed and introduced himself. "I will be overseeing your care here," he said.

You responded by extending your hand which he enclosed in both of his.

"Do you know what day of the week it is?" he asked.

You shook your head.

"How about the year?"

Again, silence. You looked slightly embarrassed. My heart ached for you.

"Where do you come from, Bill?"

"Watkins Glen," you said emphatically.

"How about squeezing my hand?" the doctor asked.

You did so.

"Okay, now squeeze both."

"Oh, I can't do that," you said, looking innocently mischievous. "That would only make you fart."

We moved out into the hallway where Doctor DeJesus told us, "You must remember that nothing he says right now is to be taken seriously. He can't help what he is saying. All of his inhibitions are down. That will get better."

I liked this man, partly because he reminded me of a young version of my father. He is courteous and projects a great sense of caring.

As we walked along the hallway, I asked him, "Doctor DeJesus, what kind of hope can you give me that my husband will make a full recovery?"

He stopped and looked deeply into my eyes. "I can't. We just don't know. His injury is serious. Sometimes they move ahead in ways we never expected; other times, they do not. I wouldn't get my hopes up that he will ever have the same mental capacity that he once had."

I had been feeling so high. But his words cut through me. I couldn't stop the tears. Art put his arm around me. "God, Doctor, my husband is so bright. If we don't have his personality, what do we have? I mean, your personality is who you are!"

Then, suddenly, I thought, no dammit! He WILL make a full recovery. That's all I have to hang onto right now—and I will hang on for dear life. I wiped up my tears, blew my nose and returned to your room. No more blubbering.

You were very agitated. "Get me out of here. I want to go home!"

Even Roz couldn't seem to settle you down. Suddenly you grabbed her and pulled her close. "I always liked 'em with big tits."

Roz took it with equanimity. This was so unlike Bill Moffett, it boggles my mind to hear you talk that way.

Just then, the head nurse came in. "Mr. Moffett, your brain is scrambled now. But we are going to get it unscrambled and we are going to get you stronger."

You smiled at her and nodded. She spoke as if you understood every word and maybe you did.

After you'd been served dinner, we left the hospital and drove down the road to the Quality Inn where I checked in. Art and Diana insisted on staying until we walked across the hotel's parking lot to a sports bar/restaurant, had dinner, and I was in my room for the night.

It is beginning to dawn on me this will be my home away from home for many weeks.

Bill and Hope aboard their sailboat, Viva, 2000.

Bill and Tim on Tim's wedding day, 2003.

Bill and Hope judging wines at a Vineyard and Winery
Management Wine Judging event, 2000.

Hope and Bill at a school reunion, 2005.

Mark, who is absent from other family photos.

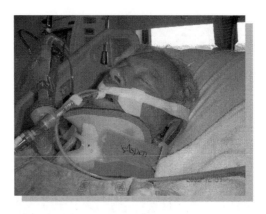

Bill, December 30, three days after the accident,
ICU, Lee Memorial Hospital, Fort Myers, Florida.

Many pictures of and from grandchildren decorated
the walls wherever Bill was.

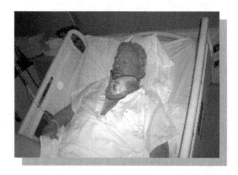

Bill, all tubes removed, ready for transfer to HealthSouth.
Lee Memorial Hospital, January 16.

Saturday, January 17

At about 8:00 a.m. I called a cab to take me to HealthSouth. Andra and Tim flew in to Cape Coral last night and will bring my car from there today. It feels strange not to be heading to Lee Memorial. I'm eager to see what the first day here will hold.

When I entered your room, I couldn't believe what I saw. There was movement under the sheet on your left side. I threw the sheet off and shouted, "Your leg! You're moving it!" You looked at me as if I had lost my mind. I forgot that when you gain back a skill you have lost, you don't seem to remember having lost it. What a wonderful way to start this day. I had believed that you would have to learn to get around with the use of just one leg. Can't wait to tell the family.

By the time I arrived, you'd had your shower, the first you have had since the accident, and were shaved. A physical therapist came in to help you get dressed—for the first time in over a month—and you seemed much more with it. You told her your name and your birth date.

The therapist, helped by a nurse, soon had you sitting on the edge of the bed, the nurse behind you preventing you from falling back. Thank goodness we could get physical therapy for you at Lee Memorial, or you probably still could not sit up. Two nurses helped you into a white golf shirt and Navy sweat pants. You looked so handsome and so normal.

Then a speech therapist arrived and tested your ability to swallow by placing small ice chips in your mouth. You can swallow, but you don't do it spontaneously. She must tell you to do it each time. She told us that this is not surprising and you will learn to swallow on your own.

She held up a toothbrush and asked you to name it. "Tombstone," you said, squinting. A tissue was a "pearl stake." You didn't seem to realize that you were not naming these things correctly. You appeared more happy and relaxed than I've seen you. There must be something to be said for having you in regular clothes. It seems to have improved your mood, your sense of yourself.

You asked to go to the bathroom and could actually do so, on a portable commode. What a relief this must be for you. You have been humiliated to have to soil your bed and then be cleaned up.

I can't believe what is being accomplished here in only one day. Getting you out of the hospital environment, working with these people who treat you with such kindness and dignity, has already wrought enormous changes.

I'm happy you looked so well when Tim and Andra arrived late afternoon. They spent two hours visiting with you, touring the facility; they were pleased with it all. When we left for the evening, Andra was determined we would have a "white tablecloth" dinner. She was sure that was just what I needed—a great dinner and a couple glasses of wine. But we found that without reservations on Saturday night, it was impossible to get a table in any of the restaurants where we stopped. I didn't have the heart to tell her I was exhausted and that my idea of a great time would be to go back to the hotel, order food from across the street and hit the sack. She did her best to find us a restaurant, but we finally ended up back at Chili's.

Back in my room finally, lying in bed, I tried to bring all that had happened into focus. My mind moved to our finances.

We are not super-rich, but we have worked hard to build a nest egg that left us comfortable moving into retirement. Now, I'm not sure how we'll pay for all of this, but I have faith we'll find a way. We own a building in Watkins Glen and if we have to sell it, so be it. I have always been the skinflint, the one nixing a purchase, saying we can't afford it. Now I feel almost reckless to spend what it will take to get you well.

Sunday, January 18

Tim came in at seven this morning so he would be with you when your private duty night nurse went off duty. You have been trying to climb out of bed and grabbing at your feed tube. The facility has a crib-type of cage that fits over the bed so patients can't climb out and can't hurt themselves, but we knew this would drive you crazy so we refused to have it used, hiring a nurse to be with you instead.

Late in the morning, Tim and Nurse Janet got you sitting up on the edge of your bed. For the first time you could balance without someone pushing your shoulders from behind. Then they moved you to a wheelchair. Wow, how good it is to see you sitting up, fully dressed, looking almost regal. We decided, what the heck, let's take you for a walk. We couldn't do that at the hospital, so this feels heady.

And how you enjoyed it! You put your face up to the sun. It has been so long since you could feel its warmth. You have always referred to yourself as "an outside dog," and you haven't been out in the air for weeks. Your feet kept falling off the foot supports and you wanted to undo your seat belt. You want to get up and walk around. I don't think I can handle this alone, but if someone else is here, two of us can manage. The kids must leave after the weekend, but Chas is returning. Now that you've been outside, I know you'll want to keep coming out. I am so glad we didn't put you in a nursing home! Here is where you belong.

Tim has been such a trooper. Tonight he kissed your forehead when it was time to leave, and said, "Dad, I love you." Then he moved behind you so you couldn't see him crying. Later that night he said, "Dad thinks kissing isn't manly, but I don't care. I am going to kiss him and tell him how much I love him from now on."

Just before we left the room, a nurse came in. You told her proudly, "My son, Tim is going to help me get out of here."

I wonder now why Lee Memorial didn't tell me about this place. I think I have a clue as I look back. I remember telling a nurse you had been accepted at HealthSouth and she said, "Oh, that's a great place! But don't tell anybody here I said so." There must be a sense of competition. I think that stinks. They weren't ready to accept you in their program, but would have been willing to let you sit in a long term care facility rather than tell us about HealthSouth. I am very grateful to so many of your caretakers at Lee Memorial and I know this wasn't their fault. But if that is a policy it should be changed.

Tomorrow your rehab program begins. It is still like a dream we are here. The atmosphere is so different from the hospital, where you were confined to your bed. Here you will attend rehab sessions and in between we can take you out for walks in your wheelchair.

Monday, January 19

You were up and dressed and in your wheelchair, very agitated, waiting to be taken to rehab when I arrived. "Let's go! I want to get going! I'm bored. This is bullshit."

Kim, one of the physical therapists who will work with you, came to take you to the gym. Your other physical therapist, Brandy, introduced herself to you and to Chas and me. Kim wheeled you in between parallel bars and said, "He will stand up today."

I'm thinking, "You're crazy! He has just begun to sit up!" These gals, neither of which tips the scale at over a hundred, can't possibly get you up, and I'm scared to death you will fall and injure one of them.

Brandy fastened a belt around your waist, then positioned herself in front of you. She pulled on the belt to help you to stand up while Kim pushed from behind. You are on your feet! Twice! You are even using the left leg that just moved two days ago. I stood with my hand tightly over my mouth, eyes bugging, I'm sure.

Then they moved you to a machine that resembles a Nordic Track, except that you sit down to use it. You did well, moving your legs as if riding a bicycle and seemed to enjoy the exercise.

Across the room, now in occupational therapy, Brandy asked you to put variously shaped pegs into holes. When she handed you a few pegs, you did exactly what you do with peanuts, cupping them in your hand, shaking them, and heading toward your mouth. She caught your hand and said, "No, these are not to eat. They fit into the holes." Once you got the idea, you did well. Your therapists are pleased with your first day's work. Part of me is inwardly cheering to see you doing so well, but the other part of me is remembering you as you once were. I am not sure whether the tears I am holding back are those of joy or grief.

When you were returned to your room Doctor Chimilewsky stopped by. You were really feeling your oats now, enough to play with the doctor.

He asked, "Bill, can you tell me the year?"

"Yes."

"Okay, tell me."

"You want to know now or later?"

"I'd like to know now."

A silence of a minute or so, as you knit your brows, trying to think. "Then I would have to say 1975."

The doctor had no way of knowing that that year had special significance for us—the year we first came together and began the magazine we published for over thirty years.

Chas and I left about 7:45, leaving your private nurse in charge. We had a quick dinner at the Ale House because we could walk there from the hotel. Neither one of us enjoys driving in the dark, especially in a strange place.

It had been a huge day—momentous. I could barely keep my eyes open by the time I got back to the room, but I knew I wanted to let everyone know about this day. Typing this all out on the computer for our CaringBridge entry seemed beyond my level of energy, so I called Kathy and told her all about what had happened. She did the entry that night to our group of family and close friends.

Tuesday, January 20

This presidential inauguration day is a sad reminder of my naiveté at the beginning of this process. I remember thinking we would watch this together and in my mind, I imagined you understanding the election of our new president. You have not come that far yet, and in your present state you hate television. The images must be confusing and you become very agitated: "Turn it off! It is just drivel!" Both of us were excited about having the first black president and were eager to see how he would do. We'd followed the debates and were impressed by his mental agility. Both of us voted for him.

Your physical therapists, Kim and Brandy have continued their gentle, yet adamant pushing. Finally, with Brandy in front and Kim behind, you put one foot in front of another the entire length of the parallel bars.

And yet another milestone: Today your catheter came out. You almost immediately fell asleep, so it must have been a constant irritation. Whenever you felt the urge to urinate, you wanted to go to the rest room. Our suggestions that it was all right to just "let it go" were insulting to you. You always looked shocked. "I'm not going to do that!" But eventually you had no choice.

What would have happened if we had placed you in a nursing home? I am afraid to consider the possibilities. Without this aggressive stimulation, I could imagine you sinking farther and farther into yourself—and away from reality.

Friday, January 23

I am in Cape Coral, having finally worked my way down through the bills, gotten all the papers signed that needed to be sent to the lawyer. A little order has been restored in a life that seemed about a millimeter from spinning out of control.

I have spent so much time running to Staples where I could have papers copied that I decided to invest in a small copier. At least then I can do it all at home.

When John and Jeanne heard that I would be away from you for a few days, they immediately formed a team of our friends, one or two of whom would visit you each day I was gone so you would have familiar faces every day. What did we do to deserve such wonderful friends?

Sunday, January 25

After John and Jeanne spent Saturday night with me, they invited me to attend Mass with them in the morning. At first the pageantry of the service deeply affected me. I realized how long I had been holding back tears. Boy, did they threaten to burst out then. Not now, I told myself and, digging my fingernails into my palms, gradually settled down. I could finally get peace and solace from the liturgy.

After the service, the Kremers headed back to their home in Fort Myers and I returned to Cape Coral to pack for my return to HealthSouth. I hate that hellish highway, Route 75, but today being Sunday the drive was a piece of cake.

When I arrived at HealthSouth, I discovered that Dimitrius had been your nurse today. He is sensitive, and strong enough to make your transfers from bed to wheelchair. You told Dimitrius you needed to have a bowel movement, but that you needed to be alone. You told him it embarrassed you to have someone with you. You don't understand the danger of this. The combination of your pants being down around your ankles and your natural instinct to stand up would surely result in a stumble and fall. There is no way we will let you hit your head again! Dimitrius has discovered that he can leave the door open just a crack, so he can peek in without you knowing you are being watched, and then just as you finish, he comes in to help you.

Doctor DeJesus said today you have reached level six on the Rancho Los Amigos scale. You were at level one when you were admitted to Lee Memorial. I was ecstatic over your progress until the doctor explained that this means HealthSouth must discharge you. What?! Again? He explained that prior to four years ago Medicare allowed rehab patients a much longer stay. Once again I have been taken by complete surprise. I assumed that you could stay here until you were at least walking on your own and your mind had cleared. Will life ever stop being a roller coaster?

I still can't handle you at home, so here we go again in a race to find another facility. The social worker brought a list of assisted living facilities. Back to this again! After I had looked through about a dozen pamphlets, she said, "There is one other place that has a pretty good reputation for working with brain-injured patients but Medicare will not foot the bill, so it would have to be self-paid. It is very expensive."

"I want to know about everything that is available. I will make the decision as to whether or not we can afford it," I told her.

As soon as the physician's assistant came on the ward, I asked her what the criteria are that decide when a patient will be discharged. "Even we don't know that," she said. "Medicare makes that decision and I think they don't want even us to know what the criteria are. It is very frustrating, but we have no choice in the matter."

Tuesday, January 27

Today is the one month anniversary of our accident. It feels as if I have lived an entire lifetime in this month. Every day seems to bring a new challenge and still the nurses tell me to steel for what is to come. "It gets worse," they say. How can it get worse?

You are now confabulating all day long—each day is a different subject.

Confabulation is when a patient fills in memory with events he accepts as facts.

Yesterday was firefighting day. "There is a fire that I have to get to! People are dying. I can hear their screams! Please don't keep me here. I have to go and save them." This goes on for hours. It was heartbreaking because you were so sincere—and panicked at not being where you imagined you needed to be.

Today it is submarines. First you are describing your "duty" aboard, feeling bad you re-upped in the Navy without telling your family. Then suddenly you are planning a trip with the kids to Minneapolis.

Bill was never a firefighter or a submariner.

I know this is part of the process, but holy hell it is hard to watch and hear. And then, just when I think I've reached the end of my rope, a part of the old you emerges through all the fog and I get a new jolt of energy.

Peter and Joette Knott visited this afternoon. When Doctor DeJesus came for his daily visit, you announced, "Doctor, these are our good friends from back home in Watkins Glen. We sail together. Peter and Joette Knott."

The doctor's eyebrows shot up as he glanced over at me.

I nodded yes.

"That's very good!" he said.

After Peter and Joette left you seemed to feel elated and asked me to take down a letter you wanted to dictate. "Dear Kids. Our next line might be about letters that are hard to write. We're thinking about you in San Francisco, frustrated that we can't be together. We love you all, and we've been thinking about coming up the Russian Sound. We need a glass of red wine! One thing that we always share is that we're part of a flock. Let's talk about getting together next weekend or the weekend after. Love, Dad"

Although this seems encouraging in the sense that you are thinking about family, it is disjointed and filled with half-truths. Nobody is in San Francisco although we have been there with some of the family in the past. You meant, I assume, the Russian River, in Sonoma County where we'd been living winters for over twenty years, since there is no Russian Sound, but the main message is still upbeat, and I know the children will recognize that. I'll e-mail it to them when I get back to the hotel.

Tonight as you sat in your wheelchair, impatiently waiting for the nurse to come in and give you your shower, you said, "There's plenty of room to feel lonesome and lonely in here, isn't there?"

I put my arms around you. "You are not alone, my friend."

"I know. I know. But sometimes it feels like that."

Wednesday, January 28

When I came in this morning your breakfast tray was still here. You had finally eaten! I think it was the grits, smothered in butter that did it. Maybe we can get rid of that damned J-peg. A J-peg is a tube that goes directly into the stomach. A cup like device is hooked to it into which liquid food is poured. The reason it was installed was because you were refusing to eat. But now I wonder if you have refused because you feel full from the liquid. A dilemma. It is strange to think that you will probably not remember any of this.

The nurses here wear nametags that not only have their names on them, but also the state in which they were born. The tag worn by the nurse who came in this morning listed New Jersey as her home state. You told her you used to live in Morristown and had been with Charles Scribner's Sons. In these moments of your rare lucidity, my heart soars.

But then she asked what you did for a living before coming here and you responded, "Construction." You paused for a minute seeming pleased with yourself. "Yep, constructed a huge recipe book."

Following Doctor DeJesus' suggestion we do not follow you down your flights of fancy, but continue to gently reorient you to the present, I said, "Remember? We published a trade publication."

"Right," you responded proudly to the nurse. "About health."

"What about grapes and wine? Remember?"

Your face suddenly became sad and you shrugged. "You'd better tell her. "I think I'm not a great story teller anymore."

That makes me wonder if I shouldn't let you go on. I'm not sure knocking the wind out of your sails is a good thing.

We "constructed" a cookbook many years ago, that we add to each Christmas for our own family and close friends. You have done all of our cooking for years and you have become an excellent cook and take great pleasure from it. You have confused this with our magazine. I decided not to make an issue.

Several weeks ago I realized that we would need a lawyer to help us figure out car insurance issues. Our son-in-law Marijn, Andra's husband, found Grossman, Roth and Partridge, trial lawyers reputed to be the best in southwest Florida specializing in representing accident victims. Their office is right here in Sarasota.

Although it takes hours each week to copy all of your medical records,

I understand how important it is that we have the hired the law firm. They have walked us through this medical jungle in which many people have gotten lost. They have discovered insurance I never would have known about.

Bill Partridge came to visit today, arriving while you were in physical therapy. When he coughed, I must have looked alarmed because he said, "Don't worry. It is just something I may be coming down with."

"Oh, Lord, the last thing I want is for Bill to get sick. Please wash your hands. And when he comes back from rehab he will want to shake your hand. Please do not touch him. And wash the pen, too, please."

Without another word, he took off his suit jacket, rolled up the sleeves of his white shirt, and scrubbed thoroughly. I was impressed on a whole new level.

I know I am getting nuts on this cleanliness issue, but I am determined you will not get sick. Your resistance is down; sickness would set us back seriously.

After he left, you were resting quietly in your bed. I was rubbing your shoulders.

You pulled me down close. "Can you tell me what happened here?"

"We were in an accident on December 27. You have been in the hospital." We talked in whispers.

"I can't remember any of it."

"I know. That is because you were thrown forward and your head hit the dashboard. You lost consciousness and you were in a coma on full life support in the hospital for several weeks."

You gazed up at me with those pale blue eyes. "I have no recollection. It seems like just a hole in my memory." Then you pulled me closer. "You are an amazing woman. We have been together for a long time. I'm so glad we have our love."

Thursday, January 29

When I came in this morning, you were sitting in your wheelchair at the nurses' station, looking very agitated, wearing only your hospital gown, which doesn't even cover the diaper you were wearing. You were scribbling on a nine by twelve sheet of paper. It was a bill, you said. You needed to pay the Schuyler County Sheriff. Signing the bottom with a flourish, you handed it to me. "There. Now you can explain this to everyone."

As a nurse walked by, you shouted, "I hope you are enjoying your freedom! This is like a jail in here."

I asked the nurse in charge, "Why isn't my husband dressed? Why has he been left out here so exposed, without even a robe?"

She looked harried. "He is scheduled to have an occupational therapist work with him today on learning how to dress himself."

"Well at least you could have him covered until she gets here."

Physician's Assistant Terry walked by just then. She dashed to the supply station and returned with a blanket she tucked in around your legs.

Later, talking to our friend Peter Honsberger I was still huffy. "Can you imagine?" I said to him.

Peter has managed several assisted living facilities in his long health care career. "I'd be careful about the fights I choose," he said. "Bill won't remember this. Think of it this way. If it will affect him in a year, fight for it. If not, it's probably better to roll with the punches. These people really do work hard."

I knew I was hearing words of wisdom. It was time to get off my high horse and pick the battles that count.

~

You were able to walk the perimeter of the gym twice this morning. Then you told your therapist you had to urinate. A male assistant took you to your own bathroom and you urinated standing up. Hurray! Gradually you are getting your dignity back. Just a few weeks ago, before your injury, who'd have thought this would be a cause for celebration?

Today has been "boat" day. You are determined to get us down to the marina to work on our boat. I explained to you that Caliloo, our 30-foot sailboat, is in Watkins Glen, and that is 1,500 miles away.

"Why do you keeping saying that? Just get me down there, will you?"

I pushed your wheelchair outside, thinking the beautiful day might be a distraction. As soon as we were out the front door you demanded to be taken to the car. This has become a major problem, so I have been parking farther and farther away. You're adamant, then pouty. "Why can't we go home? I don't understand why I have to stay here. I want to go home."

You are happiest in physical therapy where you are being kept active and occupied. Although you resented Kim and Brandy in the beginning, you have become fond of them. You will still occasionally give them a hard time. During this afternoon's session, you became annoyed when Brandy continued to help you steer your walker down the hallway. "I want your hands off!" you told her. "I want to drive on my own."

"Fine, here you go," she said and stepped aside. You kept bumping into the left wall, a reflection of your left side neglect. You were frustrated, but determined to continue by yourself.

Friday, January 30

Social Worker Jenny just came down to the room to tell me that your discharge date has been scheduled two weeks from today. My heart sinks, but then I think about how much has been accomplished in the two weeks you have been here. Who knows what the next two weeks will bring? Still, I don't dare suspend our search for another facility. I know your progress won't be steady.

Your classes these days comprise physical therapy (usually in the downstairs, larger gym), occupational therapy (which you hate and therefore resist as being beneath you) and speech therapy (which you resist almost as much and I can't blame you). The speech therapist here is a weak link. The poor soul is pregnant and can barely keep her eyes open during sessions.

You are usually bushed when you get finished with all your sessions, and need a nap. This afternoon after you'd settled into your bed, Doctor DeJesus came in for a visit. You told him you had spent the morning flying light aircraft and that I had been with you, a trusted assistant.

Doctor DeJesus gently reminded you that you are here at Health-South and had just finished your day's therapy.

You looked up at the pictures of all of our children and grandchildren hanging on the wall and some paintings the grandchildren had done. "Doctor DeJesus," you said. "You see those children. They are such a gift. I love them all so much." And you burst into tears.

Doctor DeJesus nodded and said he understood, then made a quiet exit.

You turned to me. "I am so glad you are so strong. I never would have been able to do what you have done."

You cried again. "I feel like such a baby," you blubbered.

I told you it isn't babyish to cry, just human. I held you for a few moments and I could feel you relaxing in my arms. When I pulled back a little so you could lie down, you closed your eyes and drifted off.

Tim arrived about 5:00 p.m. He'd brought his laptop, which he placed on a table. He pulled your wheelchair up to it, then pulled another chair up for himself. He brought up the CaringBridge site and pointed out the several thousand messages we have received from all over the country. You were moved. "I know all of them," you said, as Tim scrolled down. "How kind of them to write."

Tim and I drove back to Cape Coral tonight. The intimacy of the darkened car seemed to help him to open up about some issues he has apparently buried for a long time. He is so concerned about his relationship with you. He has felt distanced, for several years, and sad about that. He said, "But now Dad seems so vulnerable, and I'm feeling so close. It makes me feel guilty that we weren't this close before. Why is it that when he is strong, there is this detachment, but now I can feel my love for him?"

Saturday, January 31

Tim left me in Cape Coral to return to Sarasota at six this morning to meet Andra, arriving at the Sarasota airport around nine. With the two of them there, I will take a few days off. I plan to spend the time searching for a new facility.

When we first arrived at Lee Memorial we had been given a bag with a soft blanket, extra toothbrushes and other comforts, with a brochure for a group called "Mothers Against Brain Injury." The brochure described how this woman's son had sustained brain damage from an accident over five years ago and how she had not understood what to do. She said she wanted no one else to experience this. I thought she might be a good resource for beginning our search.

I was amazed that she answered the phone on the first ring.

She told me about a person named Adrian, an administrator at the Florida Institute for Neurologic Rehabilitation (FINR). "He knows every facility in the area," she said, "and if he thinks you aren't right for FINR he'll suggest other facilities."

Adrian, too, was easy to reach. He said he would visit you at Health-South to see if you are an appropriate candidate for his facility. "I'll be blunt," he said. "FINR is self-pay. If you tell me you can't afford it, I'll come up with some other names."

"This is how I want to work this," I told him. "I want to begin with what would be the most ideal facility available. Then I'll decide if we can afford it or not. I don't want to rule anything out at this stage." We agreed that we would make a date within the next week to visit FINR.

I'm learning we will receive more insurance than I thought possible, thanks to our lawyers. That helps me relax a little about upcoming expenses.

Tonight, I joined John, Fran, Chris and Michelle at T. J. Fridays for a birthday dinner for John, who turned eighty-one. John is still wearing his collar—and hates it. It'll be a banner day for him when it comes off. As usual, I felt awkward and strange being with the group in a kind of celebratory mood. I feel guilty feeling any joy, but these times refresh me, and I know how important it is to get breaks from the rehab routine.

Just as we were being served dessert my cell phone rang. "Where the fuck are you? The kids left and here I am alone again!"

I am getting used to these calls and learning to use my soft voice to soothe you and explain why I need to be away sometimes.

Tim and Andra joined me back in Cape Coral after their stay in Sarasota about 10:00 p.m., full of stories about their weekend with you. Mostly, they are elated at your gains. I think they want so badly to believe that you will someday be the same person you once were that every step forward seems to bring you closer.

Yet, I am not sure that they want you completely as you once were. Your needing them is a new phenomenon—and one that perhaps is bringing them to a new place in their relationship with you.

Monday, February 2

The three of us were up at 5:30 a.m. to be on the road early enough to relieve your night nurse. We stopped at the Kremers on the way because Jeanne had baked one of her famous apple pies for you. You are still not eating, and she is hoping this will whet your appetite.

Later in the morning I met Kim on the elevator. She told me a story that made us both laugh. You had been in the upstairs gym when a new patient was wheeled in. Kim pushed him over to face you. "Mr. Moffett, this is Mr. Jones. He is new here. Would you introduce yourself to him and tell him a little bit about what you did before your accident?" Kim said you looked earnest and extended your hand for a cordial shake, saying, "How do you do, Mr. Jones. I am Bill Moffett. Before my accident I was Commander of the Starship Enterprise." Kim, still laughing, said it brought the house down.

It has been discouraging and frightening trying to find a next place for you. Any skilled nursing facility we have visited or called doesn't come close to matching the rehab you are receiving here. It would be a sudden reduction in rehab at just the time you really need it to make the trip back to normal.

Tim left this morning, having used up another week's vacation, and Andra was slated to leave this afternoon. Just as she was ready to go downstairs to her cab to take her to the airport, my cell phone rang. It was Adrian. He was vehement that you should continue rehab now while your injury is still "fresh." He said if you are accepted at FINR you will get intensive rehab, building on what you have accomplished here.

While I cradled my cell phone to my shoulder, talking to Adrian, Andra and I walked to the elevator. As we reached the main front doors we could see her cab waiting.

I hung up and said, "I think this might be it—the next place for your dad," and burst into tears.

I have tried to be strong for the kids. I never intended to say goodbye that way. I was still wiping away tears and waving as her cab pulled away.

Tuesday, February 3

I was just leaving Quality Inn this morning, when my cell phone rang. It was Nurse Robin at HealthSouth. "This morning you should not come here directly," she said. "Bill was sitting at the nurse's station this morning when he suffered a seizure. Doctor DeJesus is transferring him to Doctors Hospital just to be on the safe side, although he seems fine now. Go directly to the hospital. He will be in the emergency room."

Had I received the call just two minutes earlier, I would have been able to pull out of the hotel's driveway, cross the highway and pull into Doctors Hospital. But I had turned left by the time she told me where you were headed. I had no choice but to drive all the way to HealthSouth before I could turn around and head back to the hospital.

On the way, I began to worry that you would be confused and scared. It made me want to hurry to get there, but I had to go with the flow of traffic. When I arrived you were still in the emergency room, lying on a gurney, staring at the ceiling. You didn't seem to know you were in a different setting and did not respond to my greeting.

At about 10:00 a.m. the house doctor came into our room and told me that the CAT scan showed a substantial hemorrhage on the left side of the brain. Left side!? "Has he had a fall?" he asked.

"Not that I'm aware of and he's had round the clock nursing care."

The doctor thought it certain that surgery would be necessary, but that we would have to wait for the surgeon to make that decision. The surgeon, he said, had a full schedule of surgeries today so it might be late before he could get to us.

Surgery? Just as you were making such terrific headway? I felt like my knees would give way. I e-mailed Andra. She has contacted all the other children. I also called Art and Diana, who dropped everything and were on their way here within minutes.

You were asleep, under the care of a nurse, so I went down to get a cup of coffee. Doctor DeJesus came over from HealthSouth and joined me at the table, reassuring me that if surgery is necessary, the surgeon here, Doctor Peter Mayer, is considered among the best in southwest Florida. "And you know," he said, "This resets the clock in terms of his discharge." The impact of this wouldn't hit me till later.

The day dragged on. I tried to read. I wondered if you had been sedated, because you slept all day. Art and Diana arrived in the early afternoon. Having them there helped the time pass. They tried to keep me positive and occupied. We didn't dare leave the hospital, not knowing when the surgeon would want to see us.

It was 7:00 p.m. when Doctor Mayer finally came into your room. He had taken the time to study your scan before meeting with us. He suspected that the original hematoma had gotten worse, but also remarked on the hemorrhaging on the other side of the brain, also causing pressure. There was no question about your need for surgery. He explained that he would take a section of skull out of both sides of your head to drain the blood causing the pressure. The positive side of this, he said, was that relieving the pressure might make your confusion disappear, or at least improve.

The thought of your head being drilled into was more than I could imagine. How much can your body take?

We stood in the darkened hallway. "When do you suggest surgery be performed?" I asked.

"In about twenty minutes."

I could hardly catch my breath. "Are you sure? Can't it wait until we have some time to think about it?"

"There is really no other choice that doesn't place your husband in grave danger. The longer the pressure exists, the greater the risk for permanent damage."

"I have to at least call our children."

He nodded. "That's fine. I'll wait."

Diana stayed with you, her hands full, trying to convince you to lie down. You continued to try to climb out of bed. Art came with me to the waiting room where I called Andra. Both she and Marijn agreed quickly that we had no choice and that she'd let the others know.

When we arrived back upstairs, Art said to Doctor Mayer, "Are there any questions we should be asking? At a time like this you so wish that you had better knowledge, but we don't even know enough to ask an intelligent question, except are you absolutely sure this is necessary?"

"No question," Doctor Mayer replied. "Without surgery the pressure will continue to build."

Everything was moving so fast; I felt like I was walking on a tightrope, but that if I fell off, it meant *your* life. I placed my hand on Doctor Mayer's arm. "You have been in surgery all day. You must be tired. Can you tell me that you will be able to perform this surgery at your top level of concentration?"

He smiled a kind smile. "Absolutely. This is in a day's work for me. I will be able to perform at my best."

So Diana went with you to the pre-op room, while Art and I met the team that would work with you in surgery. The anesthetist asked if there was anything I would like him to know and I told him you have been difficult to intubate. As I watched you being wheeled away I wondered if I would ever see you alive again.

I knew that as much as the doctors play down surgery, brain surgery must be at the top of the scale for danger. If you made it through, who would be left? I thought I had dealt with heavy issues before, but I had never known this weight on my heart. What if this was the wrong decision? Then, stupidly, I wondered how you would look bald.

None of us had eaten since morning so Art and Di suggested we walk over to Chili's. It was a brisk night; the ten-minute walk felt good. I was in a dream state, ready to burst into tears, trying to hold it back. Art and Di continued to be strong, accentuating the positive, holding my hand through this forest of anguish.

I have no memory of what we ate that night. Probably not a lot. I have lost ten pounds since this all began. A constant lump in my throat makes swallowing food difficult. I have tried to lose ten pounds for years—now I don't give a damn. It seems so inconsequential.

After dinner, we went right back to the hospital and had a long wait. It was 9:45 when Doctor Mayer reappeared. He said the operation had gone "all right."

That jolted me. In my experience, surgeons always tell you things went "just great." "All right" didn't sound reassuring at all.

As we'd suspected, they had trouble intubating you so they'd left the ventilator in for the night. Doctor Mayer explained that if you had trouble breathing during the night they wanted to be prepared, and didn't want to have to repeat getting the tube down your throat.

What he told me next made me feel dizzy. In the glare of the waiting room he said he had found "significant" brain damage. "You should not expect a full recovery," he said. "I believe his thinking capacity will be impaired and he may be . . . difficult."

I cried all the way back to the hotel as my brother and sister-in-law tried to comfort me, through their own tears. "Dammit, we could beat anything physical," I said. "But please give me back his brain, his beautiful, funny, fast brain. Without his brain, what is left?"

Then, from somewhere, again, I felt that jolt right up my back. No goddammit! I will not give in to pessimism. It makes no sense to do so.

You will come back! I will not stop believing in that.

In my hotel room alone I did something I hadn't done in many years. I knelt by my bed and prayed. Resting my face on the cool, soft comforter, I said, "Please God, give me strength, courage and wisdom. Please protect Bill. Please be with him."

I stayed there talking to God for a long time.

Wednesday, February 4

Art, Di and I were back at the hospital by 7:00 a.m., where you were in intensive care. The nurse said you had been quiet during the night, not surprising since the anesthetic probably had not worn off. You looked pitiful. The ventilator was back in your mouth, pulling it down. Bandages were wrapped around your head, which had been shaven. A plastic bag was on either side of your head, about ear level, collecting liquid that was draining out of the holes the surgeon had drilled. The liquid was clear with swirls of blood.

The morning quickly became a nightmare. The respiratory therapist said he needed to have you awake before removing the ventilator. But as you awakened you thought you were choking and it took two of us to hold you down and not allow you to pull the ventilator out, or your collar off. You locked eyes with Art, begging him wordlessly to help you. We took turns, two on, one off, for an hour and a half that seemed like a week. You became more and more violent. Your eyes were wide and full of anguish. You thought you were dying, unable to breathe and you were asking us to save you, but we couldn't.

Finally, finally, the respiratory therapist said it was time. The tube came out easily, one pull. I was shocked at how long it was. It looked to me about a yard. You heaved a sigh and fell back on your pillow, closing your eyes.

Art ran out to the waiting room, where I found him sobbing. "Jesus," he said. "When he looked at me like that, begging me to help and I couldn't. It just tore me up."

Saturday, February 7

Kathy has been here since Thursday. Having her has been heavenly. When she first planned this trip, she thought she would see us at HealthSouth, but now every morning we are here at Doctors Hospital by 7:00 a.m. and stay until 7:00 at night when your night nurse arrives. If we don't have someone in attendance with you constantly they put you in restraints.

Yesterday, when we arrived at the hospital, the nurse stopped us from entering your room, explaining that you had been tested for MRSA (methicillin resistant staphylococcus aureus—an infection that is resistant to regular antibiotic treatment). You have spores in your nasal passage. This does not mean you are infected, only that you might be a carrier, and that here in intensive care, we must now put on a gown and gloves before entering your room. Each time we leave, we have to remove them and discard them, putting on a new set when we re-enter. This is also true for the nurses. The damned things are paper; they're stiff and unnatural-feeling.

The good news is that you have recuperated from your surgery well. You have zipper like incisions on either side of your head just above your temple. I know the first time you see yourself in the mirror you will be shocked, but I'm amazed at how good you look bald.

You no longer need to be in intensive care but, when the doctor told me two days ago that he would transfer you to a stepdown floor and that, the next day, you would be discharged back to HealthSouth, I asked, "Why not just move him once?" He agreed if the bed in intensive care wasn't needed.

That turned out to be a bad request because the bed at HealthSouth became occupied during the night, which meant we were in limbo at Doctors Hospital waiting for you to be transferred back. Staying in intensive care is not a good idea on several fronts. First, infection is more rampant here, hence the extra care taken because of the MRSA found in your nasal passages. And also because you are hooked up to a lot of machines that you don't need but you must stay connected to while you are here in intensive care.

And it is noisy as hell in here—bells and beepers and whooshing. I can't wait to get you out.

Sunday, February 8

Kathy had to return to her home near Rochester this morning. She'd taken a week vacation to be here and now had to return to work and her husband and son. It doesn't feel as if we have really had a visit because both of us were always exhausted by the end of the day. I dreaded having her leave and being alone again. Peter and Joette had volunteered to pick her up to take her to the airport. When they arrived, I couldn't hold back the tears. Then Joette got started and we had a good cry all around. I felt desolate after they all left.

Later, while you were being given a bath, I went down to the cafeteria. I kept telling myself I would be okay, just get a little coffee down, but I felt dizzy several times.

"Damn! I can't do this!" I thought. But I couldn't seem to get ahold of myself. These 7:00 a.m. to 7:00 p.m. days, even when they're shared, are almost debilitating.

Art and Diana had only had three days at home, but when I called, Art said, "We'll be there in a couple of hours."

When they arrived, Art said, "We have an idea. I will stay here with Bill and take over your hotel room. You and Diana go to Cape Coral for a couple of days where you can catch up on your bills and get a little time off from here."

I felt like a prisoner out on leave. I was numb with fatigue, but almost giddy as Diana drove and I reclined in the passenger seat, the sun on my face. I didn't even feel guilty. I knew that Art would take great care of you. What a gift. In two days at home I could catch up on everything and I feel like a new person.

HealthSouth called this evening to say they now had a bed, so Art accompanied you tonight on your transfer.

He told us later that it was a brilliantly clear night with a full moon, and he wanted you to see it. So after you were settled back in your room at HealthSouth, he closed the door to the hallway and pushed your bed over to the window.

You said, "I feel bathed in moonlight."

Tuesday, February 10

I've returned to HealthSouth where one of our oldest and dearest friends, Raelene Shippee-Rice arrived today. She's taken a week out of her busy schedule to be with us.

Just having her here will be comforting, but thank goodness also for her medical knowledge. She is Associate Professor of Nursing at the University of New Hampshire. Added to that, her specialty in gerontology will make her inputs so valuable.

When she arrived you looked up with surprise and said, "Hey, Raelene!"

She raised her eyebrows and grinned. "You recognized me!"

You shrugged as if to say, "Why shouldn't I?"

Our friends and family don't know what to expect. How could they with your condition changing daily?

I lined up nursing care around the clock for you for the next few days because Rae and I plan to return to Cape Coral for the night. Tomorrow we have an appointment at FINR (Florida Institute for Neurologic Rehabilitation) to meet with the director, Adrian.

Thursday, February 12

We were off early this morning. Rae drove so I could spend the time on the phone talking to the lawyer's office and insurance companies. As we set out, the sun had fully risen, and it was a typically beautiful Florida day. The drive took us over country roads we hadn't seen before, flat terrain, lush with Florida vegetation. Having Rae here, and being out of the hospital for a while was helping me to relax a little.

FINR is out in the boondocks, in Wachula, Florida. The facility is impressive. In the middle of the well-appointed lobby in the main building is an ornate round table with a gigantic floral display. Plush carpeting and large paneled doors make it seem like an upscale hotel.

Adrian greeted us warmly. Gathering information from HealthSouth and Lee Memorial, Adrian had pulled together an impressive, several-pages-long, background informational sheet, with a schedule of therapies you would be involved in at FINR.

We were soon on a tour, viewing the physical, occupational and speech therapy areas. Two of the speech therapists are young women who are Ithaca College graduates. Adrian explained while we walked that you would be kept busy all day here. One of the features I think you would like is that the therapies are held in different buildings. You would be expected to walk to each, giving you a fair amount of outside time—and building strength.

A special small dining room had been set for lunch for four. We were seated with Doctor O'Keefe, a neurological psychologist on staff here, and Adrian. Adrian said to Doctor O'Keefe, "Mr. Moffett is an impressive man, even sitting in a wheelchair."

Over our salad and rolls, Adrian explained that they will ask that I leave you there alone for the first week without visiting. This, he said, would help you to learn your schedule and change your dependency from me to them.

I didn't like the sound of that even though intellectually I knew it made sense. You are very vulnerable and I'll kill anyone who hurts you.

I'm probably being paranoid but Adrian made one remark I can't forget. I told him about how you substitute words when you can't think of the right one. Once, when you wanted to lie down, you said, "This body needs to be recumbent." When I told him that, he responded by saying, "Oh, we'll take care of Mister Intellectual, all right." Something about his tone gave me the willies.

70

Rae and I drove back to Cape Coral, talking all the way about our impressions of the place and making plans for the week ahead. Rae had concerns she couldn't quite identify.

John and Fran joined us for dinner, the dinner that has become our fallback position when we are too tired to cook but we want to be together—pre-cooked chicken from Florida's biggest supermarket, Publix, served with their potato salad, beans, and wine.

We had a pleasant evening. How good it felt to be "normal." But, as always, guilt was pervasive. It felt strangely disloyal to be sitting at our dinner table with family and a friend without you. At the end of the meal, Fran said, "You know, I think I've had my fill of Publix chicken. Next time I'll even cook, Okay?"

Friday, February 13

As Rae and I cleaned up after breakfast this morning, she said, "Before we leave for Sarasota, I want to ask you something. Did you know that Bill fell at HealthSouth?"

I was stunned. "What? No, he never fell."

"Yeah, apparently he did," she said, pulling out the FINR report. "It's in here. I read through it last night. This report says he fell just two days before he was rushed to Doctors Hospital for the craniotomy after he had the seizure. This may answer why."

I was furious, scared and sad. The thought of you falling when you'd already been through so much was stunning. I had worked so hard to protect you. How could this have happened and we not be told?

Throughout the hour-and-a-half drive to Sarasota, Rae and I talked about how we would present this to Doctor DeJesus. I was ready to tear somebody's head off, but Rae suggested I take a calmer approach. "Let's see what he has to say before we go off the deep end."

It was another beautiful day in paradise that seemed to mock us. At least that's how I felt. "We should be sitting around the pool! " I thought, then, "That thinking will get you nowhere."

As we reached the entrance to HealthSouth, a van pulled in just ahead of us. When the driver of the van opened the rear door, a man got out, pushed the driver out of the way, and ran over the grassy area toward the pond. The driver spun around and ran in pursuit. Suddenly the doors to the facility opened and staff members joined the chase across the field. We pulled around the van and found a parking space.

When we reached the second floor, Doctor DeJesus was sitting at a workstation in the hallway. "I need to meet with you privately," I said to him.

He glanced up. "I'm sorry, but I'm in the middle of a crisis right now."

"How soon can you see me?"

"I don't know. I have to deal with this emergency. Then I'm due at another hospital. I don't plan to be back here till Monday."

"No, Doctor," I said. "I must see you today. My husband fell the day before he was taken to Doctors Hospital and we were never told."

He looked shocked. "I have not been aware of any fall. As soon as this emergency is over, I will look into it."

While Rae stayed with you, I went down to the cafeteria to get us both a cup of tea. When the elevator door opened on the first floor, Doctor

DeJesus was waiting, holding the man by the arm we'd seen running away. The doctor had a syringe in his hand. They stepped into the elevator as I stepped out.

An hour later, Doctor DeJesus came into the room carrying a large stack of paperwork. "These are the nurses' reports from January 31 until your husband was taken to the hospital."

He laid them on the wide windowsill with the sun shining in. He and Rae began to turn pages. I was grateful to have her eyes on them because she would know exactly what she was looking for, as I would not.

I had come to respect Doctor DeJesus so much and my anger wasn't really directed at him. I couldn't imagine him covering up a patient's fall. But I also remembered the emergency room doctor at the hospital asking me, "Has he had a fall or hit his head?" It seemed as if the evidence was very serious.

In about a half an hour Doctor DeJesus and Rae had finished poring over the charts. There wasn't a hint of a fall anywhere in the paperwork.

I pulled out my cell phone and tried to call Adrian. It was Friday night and I didn't expect him to answer, but he surprised me by doing so. "Can you tell me, please, where you got the report that Bill fell at Health-South?" I asked him.

"I'll call back in fifteen minutes. I have to review the paperwork."

My phone rang in about five minutes. "I'm so very sorry," he said. "It was a mistake. When we looked more closely at the paperwork we saw that at the top of that page, there was a woman's name. Another patient must have fallen that morning and somehow the report got mixed in with Bill's paperwork."

With my heart still pounding, I wondered: When was the last day that life was simple?

Rae's week is going by much too quickly. She has shown me new ways to care for you, been a companion to both of us. And it's even been fun going home at night, feeling like dorm sisters. It's been years since we had so much time together. She'd spent so much time with you, trying to give me a break, that a nurse who was new on the job, thought she was your wife.

Sunday, February 15

It had been a long day because there was no physical therapy so I took you to the cafeteria. I had a deck of cards and tried to think of games to play. At one point I said, "Let's separate the suits."

You rolled your eyes. "What kind of game is that?"

"It isn't a game. It's an exercise."

"I already exercised today, thank you very much." I guess I might be grateful that you have progressed enough to be sarcastic, but gratitude is not on my horizon right now.

John and Jeanne Kremer arrived about 4:00 p.m. and said they thought you had shown great gains since they saw you last, which was before your surgery. I see you every day so sometimes I don't see the gains, but it is reassuring to hear that they do. They thought you were much clearer in your thinking and were encouraged that your left side has improved so much.

Monday, February 16

When you returned after therapy today you began to take off your sneakers. I asked you to keep them on until you went to bed.

"I'm going to shower first," you said.

I explained that they only did showers at night here.

You continued to take off your sneakers. When I asked you to stop you said, "Well, then the only choice is to get them wet."

Just then a nurse entered the room and said, "Okay then, Bill, are you ready for your shower?"

Apparently, the nurse had spoken to you on your way back from P.T. Last week you wouldn't have remembered.

I feel terrible for giving you such a hard time.

The physician's assistant asked you today if you have ever heard the expression, "People who live in glass houses shouldn't throw stones?" She asked if you knew what it meant.

You deliberated for a moment and then said, "To me it means that people who are vulnerable shouldn't be doing risky things."

She was impressed and said, "Pretty close! Do you realize that means you are now doing abstract reasoning? Do you know you are getting better? Can you feel it?"

You smiled and said, "A few light bulbs are beginning to go off."

Wednesday, February 18

Even though you are beginning to have some good days and you have healed well from your surgery, the clarity of your mind is not consistent. Today you were restless so I took you for a walk in your wheelchair, thinking that might help. But your agitation elevated when we got outside.

You have a new fantasy that you are in the Navy. You think you have "re-upped" without telling us, your family. You say you feel guilty about that, but nothing can be done now. You have a date to make a speech to the parents of Navy recruits. You plan to tell them they have made a good choice for their children. You think we are in a Navy base here. *Bill was in the Navy for two years, mostly spent as hospital corpsman in Boston.*

I was very happy to see Peter and Joette arriving. Usually, having visitors is distracting and calms you down. We met them at their car in the parking lot. You seemed happy to see them and rambled on about how you have to make this engagement, this speech, and how I won't agree to take you there. We walked slowly back toward the facility. Peter took over pushing your wheelchair.

Just as we reached the entrance, I saw neighbors from Cape Coral arriving, so we stopped to wait. Once I'd introduced them to Peter and Joette, they turned to you and the shock on their faces was not well hidden. You were still rambling about your speech and it was obvious they didn't know how to respond to you. It is so hard for people who have known you before to accept what they now see.

They only stayed a few minutes.

Returning to your room, you said you needed to use the bathroom, but insisted on going in alone. Your nurse Karen went in with you anyway.

Peter, Joette and I exchanged glances as we heard you in the bathroom, yelling at the nurse.

Suddenly the bathroom door slammed open and you burst out. "I don't want that goddamned walker anymore! And the last thing I need is an obsequious nurse in the bathroom with me!"

You lurched across the room, luckily making it to the big white chair where you plopped down. You were breathing hard, bug-eyed, and very angry.

We all sat quietly for a while before I told you it was time for you to report to the gym.

No answer. You stared into space, arms crossed over your chest.

Kim came to cajole you. "You know how well you are doing, Bill. Let's keep going here."

"I am not going to have another stupid day of rehab. I want to be LEFT ALONE!"

Then, turning to me, "Get out my suitcase and pack my clothes. I am going home!"

My mind was racing. What in hell can I say that will turn this around? I thought of your incredible work ethic. "Bill, you are here to do a job. It isn't done yet. I know you and I don't think you want to walk away from this."

You are unmoved. "I won't spend another night here. It is forced incarceration."

Peter then asked you a question about something, probably sailing.

You answered him. The two of you talked for a few minutes before you said you needed a nap and fell asleep right there in the chair.

I knew that when you woke up you wouldn't remember the conversation about leaving. But it is coming up more and more frequently, and it is scary, as you gain strength and become more and more demanding.

Thursday, February 19

In occupational therapy today you couldn't grasp the concept of two and two.

No matter how Kim presented it—written on paper as two plus two equals four, or getting out four blocks and separating them into twos, then putting them together—you sat immobile, squinting, shaking your head.

You couldn't understand two and two!

She then tried a verbal challenge on the laptop. Ann wants to buy a dress. She can pay only $10.99. Question: How much can Ann pay?

Your blue eyes stared blankly at the computer screen. "Wow," you said. "This game keeps you on your toes. I'm afraid I don't know."

Oh, Baby, Baby, Baby, I ache so much for you. I ran into the hallway, crying.

Kim followed me. "Don't be down," she said. "This is how it works. You have to start way back at the very beginning. Then one day he will grasp the concept. From then on he will leap ahead. It's still in there. We just have to coax it out. Hang in there."

There has to be a special place in heaven for these workers.

The social worker here at HealthSouth had told us about a rehabilitation facility in Clearwater called Communicare that specializes in brain injuries, so I'd called. They'd agreed to visit and evaluate your case. Doctor Gordon Horn and Ron Steele, owners, came today.

When they arrived, you tried to rise up out of your wheelchair to shake hands.

Doctor Horn was impressed, but said, "Please, Mr. Moffett. Stay seated!"

You would have toppled forward if you had got out of the chair, but the courtesies you practiced all your life have a strong hold.

He asked you questions you had been asked many times before: your name, where you come from—you got those questions okay. Then, what are the year and the day? That stymied you. But then why wouldn't it? There has been little to help you remember the day of the week or the year. But I know it goes deeper than that.

You were eager to tell them about your Navy experience and what you are doing here "on base."

Ron said he was a former Navy man who was stationed in San Diego.

"That's where I was stationed!" you exclaimed, excited that finally someone seemed to understand about your Navy obligations.

You and Ron talked Navy for about 15 minutes. You beamed through the conversation.

I was alarmed this would only make your fantasy more deeply rooted. But I think neither of them understood yet that the Navy was a fantasy.

Both Ron and Doctor Horn felt you would make great headway in the next month as the blood absorbed and the irritation in your brain subsided. They agreed that it is imperative for you to continue rehab right now. "He has great reserves," Doctor Horn said. "New pathways will be formed as he recovers."

Andra arrived this afternoon to stay for a few days. She will stay here with you, so I can go back to Art and Diana's house in Brandon, which is closer to Clearwater, where we will go to visit Communicare tomorrow.

Friday, February 20

About 10:00 a.m. Art, Di and I drove past the stone wall and followed the winding driveway into Communicare. The grounds were well kept. We saw patients out walking about. We were shown a building where patients have private rooms where there is a communal living room with a large stone fireplace, surrounded by comfortable looking couches and chairs.

One of the patients, Henry, invited us into his room, to show us his computer. He is the editor of the facility newsletter. Doctor Horn imagined you might be interested in helping him and Henry is excited about the possibility of working with a former publisher of a real magazine. Though Henry seemed somewhat immature, he didn't exhibit serious symptoms of brain damage and that was heartening. I knew you would be happier surrounded by people at least close to normal.

However, as we explored further, walking out in the courtyard, we saw a young woman in a wheelchair, unable to hold her head upright, and a man with rubber boots, also in a wheelchair, noticeably drooling. I wondered what your impression would be when you got here and how you would fit in.

We walked with Doctor Horn to a group of buildings joined around a large courtyard. He explained there were ten apartments, each opening onto the courtyard. It is in one of these apartments that Doctor Horn thinks you would be most comfortable.

He unlocked the door to number 600. As we entered, we could see to the left a small living room with a burgundy leather couch, a coffee table in front and a matching chair in the corner. A television was on a table across the room. To the right were a wooden kitchen table with four chairs and a kitchen equipped with a four burner stove, refrigerator and microwave. The cupboards held a few dishes and pots and pans.

Off the living room were two bedrooms, and a bath with a walk in shower.

Ron Steele and Doctor Gallagher, founder of Communicare, joined us. Diana and I sat on the couch and Doctor Gallagher pulled wooden chairs from the kitchen table over for Art and the other doctors.

Art had come with a notebook of questions. "Doctor Horn," he said. "I'm not sure how to state this diplomatically, so I'll just spit it out. I am seeing a lot of people here who frankly look like when they get out they will be ready to be Walmart greeters at best. My brother-in-law has another destiny."

Doctor Horn smiled and said, "The fellow you met in one of the residences was a practicing lawyer before his accident. Another resident had a full scholarship to Harvard before hers. We will take good care of your brother-in-law according to his own ability, but the appearance of someone does not always tell the story."

This has been a Hail Mary. I know in my bones it is not the time to bring you home yet. I could not handle you. If the situation were reversed, it would be a different story. But with your size compared to mine, and your current lack of impulse control, it would be dangerous.

Communicare wants to admit you next Monday so it looks like another several days at HealthSouth and the Hampton Inn. I have been holding my breath to see what they will quote for a month's stay at the new facility.

Medicare had notified us that these expenses would not be covered. Why? I don't know. Do they think you have had enough rehab? Is it the services at this facility they will not cover? I don't have time to research.

I just found out it will be $1,000 a day, which takes my breath away.

Sunday, February 22

Today your frustration level is high. You don't want to be here at HealthSouth. Why can't we all understand that you are on a Navy base and you need to find the commissary so you can buy a hat?

You directed me to take you in your wheelchair to the first floor, where you indicated that we should go down the hall. You were sure we were headed to the commissary—those two doors propped open at the end of the hall.

As we approached the doors, you could look inside. You could see it was the cafeteria. "Goddammit! Take me outside."

We were not four feet outside of the entrance when you said, "Take me back in. Please, please, help me find the goddamned commissary!"

This went on all day. You couldn't concentrate on your therapies because all you could think about was the speech you were to give and the hundreds of people gathered and waiting.

I was at my wit's end, pushing you in your wheelchair up and down corridors as you searched for something connected with your Navy fantasy when Doctor DeJesus approached us on his way to see another patient.

I stopped him. "Please, Doctor, will you explain to Bill that he does not need to deliver a speech?" Often you accept his explanations, at least for a little while.

He talked earnestly to you and it seemed to calm you down.

I know this will not last, but even a few minutes of respite is welcome.

After another twelve hour day at the hospital, I am now—finally—back at the hotel.

I have brought your laundry with me, combined yours and mine and thrown two loads in the washers on the fifth floor of the hotel where there is a small laundromat.

I walk over to the restaurant across the parking lot and order a quesadilla to go. Back at the hotel, I bring a glass of Chardonnay outside to sit by the pool for a few minutes then go up to empty the washers.

I know that I am just too exhausted to run them through the drier and then make another trek up to the fifth floor. So I bring the damp clothes back to the room and hang them from every surface I can find.

Then I sit down in the middle of this strange scene of underwear hanging from lampshades to eat my cold quesadilla, feeling very sorry for myself.

Tuesday, February 24

Today you had an EEG, a follow-up to your craniotomy. We were driven to the hospital in a cab. This was the first time since the accident you had ridden in a car.

You were in seventh heaven, regaling our driver with war stories. I had to smile, sitting in the back seat, hearing how believable you were. The driver listened intently, glancing away from the road occasionally to look into your eyes.

"I'm an Admiral, but nobody calls me that anymore," you said with a touch of modesty. "Yeah, I've re-upped for special service in the Navy. Wish I'd told my wife and family first, but I didn't. Feel guilty about that, but nothing to be done about it now."

The driver seemed impressed to be driving an Admiral, especially one so down to earth.

Your EEG went fine. We had only an hour back at HealthSouth before another cab took us back to the hospital to administer your CT scan. I was very nervous about your ability to lie still long enough but that, too, went well. In fact, you fell asleep.

Back at HealthSouth you obsessed again. You wanted to go outside, where you become very agitated.

"We are going out for dinner tonight," you railed, as I pushed your wheelchair over the sidewalk outside the facility. "I am not eating one more fucking hospital meal. They don't own our nights! Take me over there. Now turn here. There! That is where I'm supposed to be giving the speech. Across the road."

"Bill, there is no crosswalk here and we can't go across the road. It would be too dangerous."

"If you won't take me, I'll get over there on my own." You unsnapped your wheelchair belt and tried to climb out of the chair.

I threw my arm around you from behind, pulling you back into the chair, and quickly came around to the front to refasten your belt.

Now I was angry. "You will NOT get out of this chair and if I can't trust you to stay in your chair, I will not bring you outside again!"

Making a U-turn, I made our way back as fast as I could walk and push you, sputtering all the way. "I've had enough of this! I can't handle this anymore. You are driving ME crazy."

As we walked through the lobby at the facility, you grabbed on to the reception desk, stopping our progress to the elevators. Pulling yourself up with dignity, you said to the receptionist, "We are not going back in here. We are going out for dinner and I am driving! She doesn't get it. I need a new driver for this chair!"

The receptionist laughed. "Honey, you can't get another driver. That woman there—you promised to stay with her for life!"

The few waiting on chairs in the foyer, found the scene hilarious.

I did not.

When we got back to your room, reruns of "Mash" were playing on the TV set. You became engrossed and laughed heartily. Then you drifted off for a few minutes and when you awoke, you were in an entirely different place, content to lie in bed and rest. Never know . . .

Good news. The results of the EEG and the CT scans show no more bleeding! I have been terrified that you would need to go back for another craniotomy. Your behavior has been so erratic that even Kim and Brandy worried there was more bleeding, causing irritation. Thank you, Lord.

Tonight, back in the hotel room, I set up my computer, pour my glass of wine, and open e-mail. There is a message from Jeanne. She has found information on the side effects of Dilantin, the drug begun after your seizure: lack of judgement, backsliding intellect, mood swings. I can hardly wait to run this past Doctor Dejesus in the morning.

The next e-mail is from Suzanne from the office of the magazine in California that we published for thirty-five years. Our son is now the publisher and owner. Suzanne said they had a little space in the Wineries Unlimited conference program and wanted to run a piece about you and a report on the accident, with an update on your health.

She sent the photo they wish to include. It is one of you at the podium at one of the conferences we sponsored a few years ago. You are holding up a glass of wine, proposing a toast. It is a picture I adore. I realize this is what you have been longing to get back to. You just have it all mixed up in your poor brain with the Navy.

I have the longest, worst, crying jag I can remember.

Sunday, March 1

Today you began your perseverating again about the Navy and I had what I thought was a brilliant idea.

I went to Walmart and bought a tape recorder. Maybe I can convince you to tape your speech and let the parents of the recruits hear it that way. (This is beginning to seem real!)

But you dismissed the idea completely. You won't even open the package, saying, "I'll open it when I get home."

John and Jeanne came today about 3:00. You had several hours of the most lucid conversation you have had since the accident.

I mentioned that the garage door wasn't working back in Cape Coral. You said, "That's probably the motion sensor." And you told me how to fix it! And for just a moment I felt like we were a couple again.

But the fact is tomorrow we transfer to Communicare. It's hard to believe that we have to adjust to an entirely different atmosphere. I can't help but be nervous about it.

When I discovered that we would have to pay for your care out-of-pocket, I asked if we couldn't stay right here at HealthSouth, where you are progressing so well.

But the word came back. Nope. Medicare says if you have used their service at a facility, you cannot become a private pay patient. Why? Who knows?

But we have been so lucky. Not only have we had fantastic support from our family and friends, we have been told that most of the churches in Schuyler County are praying for you regularly. This amazes us because neither of us has been a "go to church" person for many years.

One day we had a package from Watkins Glen and were surprised to find a maroon wool "prayer shawl" that some of the women from St. Mary's of the Lake Roman Catholic Church had knitted.

Mary Ann Marks had sent it. She explained that in their small group, they gather every week to knit or crochet these shawls. As they do, they hold the picture of the person for whom they are making it, in their minds. She said they hoped that when the shawl arrived and was placed around your shoulders, you could feel the loving embrace of all who had worked on the shawl.

We were very moved and grateful. As we talked about the prayers offered for us, I said to you, "You know, I can almost feel the power that is coming from that. Sometimes I feel as if we are being held in the palm of God's hand."

You nodded and said, "I feel it, too."

Monday, March 2

Doctor Horn arrived at HealthSouth at about 9:00 a.m. I had you all packed and ready to go. You were excited about getting out of here.

Doctor Horn accompanied us to a follow-up appointment with Doctor Mayer at Doctors Hospital, and the news was all good. There are no more sign of fluids on your brain.

It was another idyllic Florida day. Doctor Horn suggested we go to Chili's for lunch before heading for Clearwater. You ordered a large portion of ribs, french fries and chili. This is the first restaurant meal you have had and you were ecstatic.

After lunch, we headed to Communicare, you riding with Doctor Horn, and I following as we made our way over the stunning Sun Beltway, a long high span of bridge with a spectacular view of Tampa Bay beneath. On this day, the sparkling water was almost blinding.

In about forty-five minutes we pulled into Communicare's tree lined driveway. Doctor Galloway and Ron Steele came to welcome you to your new apartment. Ron brought the paperwork that needed signing. When I sat on the couch to read it, you looked over my shoulder, then came around the couch and sat next to me, staring and shaking your head, indicating you wanted to say something in private. I asked the others if we might have a few minutes alone.

As soon as everyone was out the door, you raged. "Are you crazy? Get us out of here! We could stay at a first class hotel for a third that price. We can get on a bus right now and get the hell out of here. This is outrageous. Stupid!"

I was trying to stay calm, though, I too was daunted by the expense we were incurring. "This is a place that is going to give you the specialized care you need right now. It is where we need to be."

"You're nuts!" You turned away to go sit at the table, your face in your hands. You seemed so lucid that I wondered if I HAVE made a mistake. If so, it was huge. $1,000 a day will add up fast.

The doctors returned and all of us tried to calm you, to explain how much you need the help they can give you. You finally agreed to spend the night.

So here I am at the La Quinta Hotel with the festive lighted trees and fountain cascading into the pool, all of which seems to mock my sadness. "Here you are, Hope, in Clearwater, Florida, with your husband in the rehab center down the road babbling about the Navy. Have fun!"

My room is on the pool, sought after if you are a mom and dad with kids, but in my case meaning I have to keep the drapes closed all the time unless I wish to be observed.

That makes the room as dark as my thoughts.

Tuesday, March 3

When I arrived at Communicare at 7:00 a.m. you were raging. "I'm not going to stay here another night! I was cold last night, and the bed crackles every time I move. This is no place for me! Please, Hope, get me out of here. I hate it here."

I called Ron Steele, who came to your apartment immediately. I asked him to lie down on your cot, obviously fitted with a waterproof mattress pad.

"Would you like to sleep there?" I asked him. "Especially if you were cold? Why was it cold in this room all night?"

Steele explained that a new thermostat had just been installed. Apparently no one knew how to operate it. He called the maintenance manager, who appeared with a different, simpler version. Ben Pulfer, a gentle giant of a man, who is Patient Liaison, bought you a double bed with some soft bed coverings.

The new bedclothes did not change your mind about staying here. You are trying so hard to control your own destiny—and so angry with me, who you think is trying to keep you a prisoner in a place you hate.

You slammed around the apartment, were sullen and uncooperative when various staff members came in to introduce you to the routine you'll be following.

One of the providers walked in without knocking and you were furious. "Didn't you ever learn to knock before entering?" you shouted.

This is apparently their modus operandi, knock then walk in. But, I told Ron Steele to please ask caregivers to knock and wait for a response before entering.

This did not mollify you. "Why are you staying in a posh hotel and I have to stay here? If you think this is such a great place to be, why aren't you staying here?"

About noon, you shouted, "I have had it! If you won't take me out of here, I will go by myself." You slammed out the door and headed across the property.

Following you, I said to a nearby caretaker, "Get help."

As you got close to the busy street, I stood in front of you. "You cannot go into this street! This behavior is unacceptable."

I had never been afraid of you physically before, but the difference in our size was now so evident. I could see staff members, taking up positions behind bushes and posts.

Doctor Horn strolled toward us. "Hi Bill," he said softly.

"Yeah. Hi. Get me out of here, will you?"

"Where do you want to go?"

"I want to go to Hope's hotel."

"Okay, we can do that. Come on. Follow me."

He walked back across the property, steering you gently by the elbow. Is he going to take you back to the hotel? What if you escape later and try to run there?"

He got into the driver's seat and motioned you into the passenger side. I slid in the back. We edged out to Route 19, while Doctor Horn kept up a steady dialogue with you, asking you questions, sometimes laughing.

And then you were laughing, too. You suddenly seemed to be enjoying this little hiatus.

We parked next to the pool at the hotel and walked through the gate toward my room. I unlocked the door and we all entered. The drapes were drawn, so the room was darkened.

Doctor Horn said, "Bill, why don't you just lie down on this bed and rest. It is quiet here. Maybe you can just veg out."

You lay down.

I perched on the edge of the other bed, wondering what in heaven's name would happen next.

"I'm going to leave you two alone for a few moments while I make a couple of phone calls," Doctor Horn said. "I'll be back in a few minutes."

You were quiet, staring at the ceiling. I said nothing. I decided not to move an inch because I had no idea how you would react. Suddenly you turned on your side, away from me.

When Doctor Horn returned you said to him, "Why can she have such great quarters and I have to stay back there? This is really pissing me off!"

Doctor Horn, stretched out on the bed next to you, cradling his head in his hand, facing you. "Here's why, Buddy. You have work to do so you can get back to living your life." His voice was low, very gentle— and in that moment I knew I had taken you to the right place.

Within ten minutes he had calmed you down. We slowly got up to return to Communicare.

When we walked in the door to your apartment, you walked through the kitchen, and then stopped, appearing confused.

"There is supposed to be another door here and I want to lock it."

Shaking your head as if to clear it, you turned and walked into the living room.

Finally, you settled down on the couch and opened a Michael Creighton book. You looked so perfectly normal. You have been doing more and more reading lately. I have no idea if you remember what you have read.

Wednesday, March 4

You are trying so hard to rise to the surface through what must feel like thick fog.

From the time I arrive, you want my attention every moment. You seem unable to experience empathy, so my being exhausted means nothing to you. You want me to rub your feet to help you get to sleep, to sit next to you while you read, to get you coffee.

You are certain today we are in Lodi, New York. You get angry when I explain that we are in Clearwater, Florida. "Please don't confuse me like this! Why do you keep insisting we are in a place called Clearwater? You want to keep me confused, don't you?"

"No, Bill, I do not. I just want you to understand where you are."

"Oh, please don't start that again. I don't get why you are purposely trying to confuse me."

More and more you are treating me like an enemy. I'll have to ask one of the doctors if this is normal, something brain-injured patients routinely do.

My original plan had been to spend a few days getting you settled in here, and then taking some time in Cape Coral. You have twenty-four hour supervision here. Maybe, I thought, I would sleep for about forty-eight hours.

But when I explained to Doctor Horn my plans to leave, he asked that I stay through the first weekend. "There is no planned therapy over the weekend," he explained. "You will have the chance to take him out somewhere if you wish. The caretaker can take one of our cars. It would be pretty hard for him without you right now."

So I agreed to stay until Monday, then spent one more day because you had a scheduled cooking test with an occupational therapist Monday afternoon.

Even though the cafeteria is a few steps away from your apartment, you have asked to cook for yourself in your apartment. The staff wants to be sure you will be safe doing so.

Monday, March 9

The OT arrived about 3:00 p.m. After a few minutes of small talk, she said, "OK, let's get to work. Let's see if you can cook a meal."

For the last 20 years Bill has done all of the cooking at home. He enjoyed studying new techniques which he tried out at dinner parties for friends. Our shelves are crowded with cookbooks and old issues of Bon Appétit, Cooks Illustrated magazine, and many more. I remember John Kremer saying once, "When Bill invites you to dinner, don't refuse!" Not only were our dinner parties famous for good food, but for elegant presentation.

Today, you removed canned tomatoes, canned beans and ground beef from the cupboard, then placed them on the counter next to the stove. I had taken you to Publix this morning to get the ingredients on the list that you'd spent hours putting together. Your plan was to make chili.

You chopped up about half an onion then, began to sauté the beef. As it browned, you added the onion, the tomato sauce and the beans. The cooking aroma filled the apartment.

Then you stopped suddenly and, staring into the pan, shook your head.

You came over and sat next to me on the couch. Cupping your hand around my ear, you whispered, "I am lost here. I can't seem to figure out where to go next."

The OT said, "Bill, come on. It's time to get creative."

I squeezed my eyes tightly to keep from crying. I can't help. I can't help . . .

You returned to the stove and stirred together the ingredients. Then you went to the cupboard and pulled out a can of ready-made chili, opened it, and poured it into the pan. When everything had heated through, you dished it into three bowls.

"Well, Bill, you pulled it off," said the OT. "I will say you are all right to use your stove and cook in your apartment."

You beamed.

When she left, you exhaled a huge sigh as if you had been holding your breath. "Whew, I think she was easy on me, don't you? I mean I really lost my way there and she gave me a second chance."

"You did great!" I gave you a big hug.

You looked sheepish and little boyish.

I felt like crying.

93

Tuesday, March 10

Today caretaker Gina drove us to Macaroni's for lunch. You ordered the seared scallop salad, proclaiming it to be the best scallops you have had in a long time. You looked very handsome and were, as always, glad to be dining out. You graciously offered both of us tastes of your lunch. Anyone sitting next to us in the restaurant would have thought us to be a normal threesome—a mother, father and daughter—not a patient with traumatic brain injury, his wife and his nurse.

On the way back you sat in the passenger seat next to Gina. Suddenly you said loudly, turning your head as if talking to someone in the back seat, "How long are you and John staying, Allison?"

Gina looked perplexed. "Are you talking to me?"

You turned all the way around and saw me sitting alone in the back seat. Turning back forward, you sat up straight and said, "I was talking to someone who is not in this car." Then pensively, "I could have sworn Allison and John were with us."

More than once, I have had memories of the movie, *A Beautiful Mind.*

Your brain seems to try to put pieces of a complicated puzzle together. Sometimes the pieces fit and sometimes they don't and you try to power them in. Sometimes you just screw up your face and gaze into the distance.

Wednesday, March 11

When I arrived this morning, Gina met me at the door. "He is really out of it this morning. Be prepared."

You were sitting on the couch surrounded by your bags full of clothes. "I am getting out of this fucking place. I cannot stay another minute. Last night somebody was hanging around outside looking like he would break in. I told the caretaker that he should call the police. Get an armed guard! I was scared to death! Lights went off. Cats were fighting. I didn't sleep a wink!"

I sat down next to you and tried my best to speak quietly and gently to bring you down, as Doctor Horn has taught me, but you shrugged me off. You were closer to hysteria than I had ever seen you.

You picked up your bags, and slamming out the door shouted that you would call a cab.

Once again I said to Gina, "Get help," and followed you, trying to talk you down.

By the time we got to the road, Doctor Horn had caught up with us. I could see other staff members, once again getting into position out of sight.

In about fifteen minutes, Doctor Horn had talked you into returning to your apartment. "His meds will kick in soon," he told me. "It will get better."

Thursday, March 12

Today your anxiety seems to have lessened. When you tried to warm leftovers for lunch, you had difficulty turning burners off and on, leaving the one on you wanted to turn off, and turning the one off you wanted to use. But instead of getting angry, you said, "Maybe I do have some fuzz on my brain. I seem to be lost here."

At times like this I want to take you in my arms and hold you, but you are not comfortable with that—with being treated "like a baby." So I settled for saying, "It's okay, Babe. It will get better."

After lunch you said you were going to take a nap. "Would you like to lie down with me?" you asked.

I climbed in next to you and put my head on your shoulder as we have slept together for years. It felt wonderful.

But within ten minutes you rolled over, away from me, and fell asleep.

I got up and went into the living room. I would try to read a book.

Friday, March 13

My cell phone rang at 6:00 a.m. It was Ben, asking if I could get back to the facility fast. He said that you were very agitated. You had not been able to sleep, and had called Ben at home in the middle of the night. He was with you, trying to calm you down.

I got there in about 20 minutes.

You had everything thrown into your suitcase once again. When I walked in the door, you yelled, "Gotta get out of here. This fucking place is a madhouse. I don't want you here. This place is dangerous! Did you have to present papers to get in?"

I sat next to you and said, "You know, I'm hungry. How about some breakfast?"

You looked confused for a minute and then said, "Sure."

Ben smiled, shook his head and left.

I guess I'm getting good at this. Small pleasure. I have thought about how I could feel the heroine when you were still bedridden. The nurses had told me it would get much worse. At the time I had no way of knowing what they meant.

Some days now, I feel as if I am barely holding onto reality.

You put bacon in a pan, and as soon as it rendered grease, you added two eggs. Over that you poured grated cheese and chipotle pepper. Then you turned the mess out onto two plates. You ate hungrily, while I pretended to eat, worrying about what disease we were picking up from undercooked bacon and almost raw eggs.

After breakfast, your vile mood returned. "You patronize me and I can't stand it. You're never here when I need you. I'm sick to death of Ronald."

Ronald is about our age. We thought he was a present from heaven when he first became your weekend caretaker. He is a licensed sailboat pilot who has sailed a great deal and has many opinions on what is happening in the world today. He used to bring you into lively discussions that seemed to allow you to burn off steam in a positive way. He agreed to work double shifts over the weekend so you wouldn't have to get used to another person. He lives in nearby Tarpon Springs and has been eager to take us to restaurants he thought we'd enjoy on weekends when you had no therapy schedule.

But one night something happened that set you off. You had gotten up to go to the bathroom. Ronald was in your bathroom replacing the toilet paper roll and you were startled. That did it. "Get out!" you yelled. "Don't be sneaking around my apartment in the middle of the night!"

Saturday, March 14

This morning you were furious. "Get me out of here. I want to go somewhere."

I told you our friends from New York Dave and Carol Kunzmann were due to arrive for a visit within minutes.

"I don't care. I want to get out of here."

You saw I wasn't moving for the door, so you slammed into the bedroom, yelling, "If you won't go now, wake me when you're ready."

I went outside to meet our visitors at the picnic table in the middle of the courtyard.

In about ten minutes you emerged and graciously shook hands all around.

You and David sat on the swing together where you regaled him with Navy stories. Carol and I stayed at the picnic table, not sure, I guess, what to talk about. Dave and Carol have been our friends for many years. He was your membership sponsor in Lions Club and we have taken many sailboat trips together. They know you well, but have never seen you like this.

After Dave and Carol left, you called me into your bedroom and shut the door. "I think you and Ronald are becoming a couple and I'm on the outside. I have told him I do not want him in this apartment."

"Oh, Babe, never think that. It is you and I who are the couple. Ronald is a caregiver here to help."

"Well, I don't think so. I am not a couple with you. You have not listened to my concerns for the last two weeks. I want to go home to Watkins Glen. Now."

"Babe, Watkins Glen is 1,500 miles away."

Suddenly you looked threatening. I have never seen that look on your face before. You stood up and hovered over me. "I am going to knock your head off!"

Should I call for help? Should I scream?

I stood up and pushed past you. "You're not going to knock anybody's head off. Cool down!"

I didn't look back, but knew that you weren't following me and the next thing I knew you were sitting in the chair in your room reading a book.

This is the first time you have threatened me directly and it has left me shaken.

You hate all the other residents, referring to them as "druggies." You have been rude and nasty with just about anyone with whom you have been in contact, except those you view as authority figures: Doctor Horn, Doctor Tanner, the neurologist who sits in on weekly meetings, and John Gallagher, your psychologist.

Ronald and I have to sneak discussions about your care now, lest you think we are plotting against you, or having an affair. Weekends have changed dramatically. Since you are mad at Ronald, we have stopped taking trips to interesting local spots. In all of our years together I never remember you being jealous of another man, nor did I ever give you reason to be.

Now that I am the driver our dining opportunities have shrunk. I am not comfortable driving to a distant restaurant alone with you. There are plenty of restaurants nearby that I will drive to but you dismiss all of them as "pedestrian." You don't want to eat in the cafeteria though the food is very good. It is the ambiance, being with the other patients, you abhor. And I can't say I blame you for that. You are fighting with all your might to stay what you consider "normal." Sitting in the cafeteria when one of the residents is fed a pail of food, which he spoons to his mouth, getting most of it, but not all, is disheartening. Others must be fed by their caretakers. You do not understand why you have been placed in this environment.

This evening I suggested we have dinner at Sam Seltzer's, a short drive up Route 19.

"I know you think eating at Sam Seltzer's is a special treat, but believe me, it isn't," you sneered.

I wanted to knock YOUR head off!

I asked the cafeteria to send dinner over, thinking that you could take it or leave it, as far as I was concerned.

You sat down and ate heartily as if we have never had this conversation.

It bothers you deeply that you can't drink wine with meals, or any other form of alcohol.

Wine with food has been our theme for so many years. It was our profession. It was our life. We traveled all over the country judging wine.

Being in a restaurant where it is available, but you can't have any, is very difficult for you. But the doctors have been clear. Alcohol and brain injury do not mix. Your brain is working to form new pathways and they believe that alcohol will interfere with that. Nobody knows for sure what the effect of alcohol is on injured brain cells.

After dinner I was thinking that I should get out of there and leave you to your caretakers. You were becoming increasingly hostile. You see me as standing between you and your escape to normalcy, which you imagine is home.

You were wandering around the apartment, pulling out drawers, opening cupboards.

"What are you looking for?" I asked.

"Keys to the fucking Mercedes."

"The Mercedes is in Cape Coral."

"Fucking stupid."

You walked out to the Ford Explorer I had driven that day and sat in the passenger seat, sulking for about fifteen minutes. Then you got out and yelled that you were going for a walk.

You called to Ronald over your shoulder. "Don't you go into my apartment while I am gone. You stay out of my apartment!"

Ronald stood to follow you as unobtrusively as he could. It is his job—and it has become a very unpleasant one.

Tonight I called Andra and spilled my guts and now I'm sorry I did. There's nothing she can do from Boston.

Sunday, March 15

Ronald called my cell at 7:00 a.m. Since we set the clocks ahead during the night, it was 6:00, but I was awake. "Can you come here right away," he said. "He is obsessing over his speech, ran out into the parking lot looking for you, and when he couldn't find the car, or you . . . well, he is very upset."

When I got to the apartment, I joined you on the couch.

You turned to me, eyes blazing, "What the fuck?" Where the fuck have you been? I have to make a speech and you don't seem to give a fuck. Are you going to help me with this or not?"

Could I manage my "calming down" voice again?

"Remember, we made the decision yesterday that you would not give that speech. We decided that we'd been jerked around enough and that we are retired. We deserve peace. Remember?"

You reached past me for the phone on the table at the end of the couch and dialed God-only-knows whose number. Whoever answered heard, "I will NOT be presenting today!" And you slammed the phone down. You continued sitting on the couch, breathing heavily, as if you were exhausted.

I went out to the kitchen and prepared us bacon and eggs—fully cooked, that you seemed to enjoy, and then you retired to your bedroom for a nap.

When you awoke you went out in the courtyard to sit on the swing in the sun, rocked for twenty minutes, and then came back in the apartment.

"Are you ready for lunch?" I asked. You had talked to Ronald that morning about driving out to the Coast and having a nice meal at the Columbia. Apparently the prospect of having lunch on the water supersedes your hatred of Ronald today.

But another switch. "Lunch? I have too much to do. I have to report to the stadium. They are expecting me. I cannot let them down."

"Bill, remember, we decided to let this go."

"No. If you don't want to come with me—fine. I'll take a bus off base. If I don't appear now as I have promised, I may never be asked again to give a speech. Why don't you go and ask Ronald. He is ex-military. See if he thinks they will ever ask me again."

I opened the door, and asked Ronald, who was sitting on the bench, to come in. "We have something to—"

"I said you should ask him confidentially! Out of my earshot!"

Ronald and I trekked back outside. Ronald said loud enough for you to hear, "I am certain that with Bill's outstanding record and the straightforwardness he has always displayed, he would be invited back again. Besides that, officers understand when someone has his schedule interrupted."

"Good!" you say from inside the apartment. "But I still need to hear from Kirk." (Your occasional name for Doctor Horn)

So I went to the phone, and while holding down the lever, dialed. Then I had a "conversation" with Doctor Horn. "So you agree then that Bill is off the hook as far as the speech is concerned. Okay. Thanks very much."

I was breaking every rule that Doctor DeJesus had laid out concerning not going down your path, but I couldn't figure out any other way to get you out of this obsession.

Finally, you agreed to go out for lunch. Instead of the Columbia, Ronald suggested that Tarpon Springs would be a new experience and fun to see. God only knows we can use some of that.

When we got there, I wondered if Ronald had taken leave of his senses. How in the hell had he picked this place? There was a tiny, narrow street, teeming with tourists. We had to walk shoulder to shoulder. I prayed that you wouldn't punch someone if they accidentally bumped into you. There were children screaming, darting in and out of the crowd, tourists yelling to one another. This was insane.

Inside the restaurant we were seated next to a large group, having a great time, being so loud we could hardly hear one another talk. I was thinking that at any moment you would get up and walk out, but you got through lunch without incident.

As we emerged from the restaurant you realized there was a marina across the street and you walked over to look at the boats. You took off at a good pace, Ronald and me in pursuit. Before lunch you had said your legs were tired, but now we are walking farther and farther away from the car.

"Take a look at that thirty," you said. "Reminds me of our Caliloo."

I was so worried that you would get so tired we wouldn't be able to get you back to the car that I was not registering much of what you were saying. I was thinking that anyone watching us would think I was the crazy person. You were just the good-natured old salt guy having a good time, and there was his sourpuss wife trying to get him to leave, when he was having such fun.

Finally, we got to a bench, where you sat down and suggested that Ronald go get the car and come to pick us up here. Oh, if only I'd known about that bench, I could have enjoyed the stroll down the docks!

As soon as we returned to the apartment, you rushed into the bedroom to lie down for a nap. It only lasted about 15 minutes. When you awoke, you moved to your chair in the bedroom where you sat paging through your notebook—looking so "Bill." Sometimes this is the hardest, when I can imagine us being normal and we are so . . . not.

Back at La Quinta tonight, I lie in bed trying to reflect, to be sure I am making wise decisions.

You want so badly to come here to the hotel and you resent that I am here. It makes me feel terrible. But you are still having night incontinence. You are up almost every hour, disoriented, often going outside. Your caretaker has walked the perimeter of the facility with you, at 3:00 a.m. You are impulsive and angry if your wants are thwarted . . . No, I couldn't handle that at home. You really need more therapy.

Tonight I have such tender feelings for you. What must it be like to be inside your head right now—Mr. Control—who suddenly has no control at all?

I pray for a long time. "Please, Bill, come back."

Monday, March 16

Another early morning call, this one from Gina. It was still dark. You wanted me. I was ready to go anyhow.

When I arrived, your clothes were all over your bed, some packed in a pillowcase, every piece of clothing pulled out of your closet and drawers.

I convinced you to go to the cafeteria for breakfast, but when we returned you refused to put your clothes away. We had a weekly meeting scheduled for 10:00 a.m. with the entire staff. So we left the apartment in shambles and walked to the administration building.

In the meeting, you held court as if you were conducting a staff meeting, as you have done hundreds of times. "I think my meds should be reviewed. The medicine to keep me peeing is also keeping me awake all night. Also the Seroquel is making me very sleepy in the morning. Why not try only a nighttime dose?"

Where in hell did this come from? Are you being "crazy" just when you are with me; can you summon up this normal Bill at will? But there you sat, looking regal, and I smiled at Doctor Tanner, who returned the smile.

"How are you seeing things, Hope?" he asked.

"Well, I think we are finally getting past the Navy thing. There are certainly still some issues, but I think we have made great strides here. I am encouraged." I didn't realize I felt that way, I guess, until I said it.

Then you chimed in. "Yes, it is great that I will finally be making this presentation. I have been looking forward to it for a long time. I'm glad to be telling the parents of the recruits that they have made a good decision to let their children join the Navy. The Navy will take good care of them—"

I jumped up and moved out to the hallway where I stood sobbing for a few minutes. Damn! I thought we were past that. I really did!

After the meeting, I had the unpleasant chore of telling you I will leave for a few days.

The staff here says it is imperative I do this—for me and for you. They say you should bond with your caretakers and depend on them, rather than on me. They say we have to reset our relationship back to husband and wife.

Art and Di have suggested that I come to their house for a few days. Art reminded me that when I go back to Cape Coral I spend all of the

105

time catching up on bills. He wants me to take two days off. I have gratefully accepted.

Being at Art and Di's this evening has been heavenly. Art grilled steaks for dinner and Diana made a beautiful salad and baked potatoes. After dinner I spent time on CaringBridge on the computer while they went out with their walking group. When they returned we retired to the family room to watch, of all things, *Dancing with the Stars*. I immersed myself in the warmth of family and normalcy.

We were just about ready to go to bed when the phone rang. It was Ben Pulfer from Communicare.

"Don't panic," Ben said, "but we have an issue here. Bill fell out of bed, got his feet tangled in the sheet, and hit his head on the floor. He has a cut over his right eye. It doesn't look bad, only superficial. Rotanda is with him. They will take him to the hospital."

I felt as if somebody had just pushed me off a six-story building and I was in free fall. This is the first time I have left you since the transfer! Hit in the head? Oh, no, please God. Not another hit in the head. "Ben, damn!" And I begin to cry.

"I knew you would feel like that," Ben said. "If you think you have to be here, I will come to pick you up. But, I'll tell you, Rotanda says he is lucid and she thinks he will be fine."

I was touched by this offer, since it would have meant several hours of driving late at night for Ben, who is a young man with a family. I told him where I was and that if we decided to go to the hospital, Art and Diana would drive me.

I wanted to take off immediately, but Art, with his level head, said, "Let's wait a few minutes. It is late and dark and we are all tired. Bill is being taken good care of. Maybe we should wait to see how he does."

We waited until about 11:00, then went to bed.

I kept my cell phone right next to me. I have gotten used to opening my eyes and seeing that phone perched on the pillow.

Rotanda called at 1:00 a.m. She said that an x-ray had revealed no internal bleeding. She was still at the hospital with you, and she said she would keep me posted.

Three a.m. She called again. She's about to go home. You are back in your apartment, sleeping soundly.

Tuesday, March 17

B en called in the morning to report you were very lucid and having a great day, joking about your stitches scaring people off. On the way home from the hospital you'd told Rotanda how hungry you were, so she stopped at McDonalds. The two of you had apparently had a meal together back at your apartment and today you're buddies.

Later, Ron Steele and Doctor Horn called to report how well you were doing. Maybe I should stay away more.

Being with you as much as is good for you, but leaving for enough time to be good for me—and for you—is an incredible balancing act. You long to have me there all the time, but I think I become a distraction, keeping you from bonding with your teachers and caretakers.

I have to return to Cape Coral before coming back to you.

Wednesday, March 18

When I awoke this morning at home in Cape Coral I had a premonition. I called Communicare to check on how you did yesterday. Brie, the receptionist, told me you and Gina had gone out to the Tuscan Restaurant for lunch.

Sitting here in bed I had this sudden thought, "Oh great, all I need is for you to fall in love with Gina."

Where did that come from?

Thursday, March 19

Today I got back to Communicare just in time for your physical therapy session with Phong (pronounced "Fawn"). She has been coming each morning and the two of you walk the property. She gives you special exercises and challenges—like stepping over logs, walking over uneven ground.

She is very attractive, Asian, tall and willowy. On her first visit to you, she explained what she wanted you to do.

"I think that's boring and I won't do it," you said.

"Yes, you will," she said. "If you wish to get better, you will do as I say."

You put your face right in hers and shouted, "You can't make me do anything I don't want to do. Now get out of here!"

She was not intimidated.

I was amazed. *I* was intimidated!

"You and I have work to do," she said. "And the next time I come back, we will begin."

Within a few days you were walking with her every day and had developed great respect for her wisdom and knowledge.

Friday, March 20

My cell phone rang in my hotel room at 5:00 a.m. "Give me Andra's number. I have to find out what her rank is . . . and Marijn's, too.

"Bill, Andra is not in the Navy."

"She isn't? Well, I have to tell you I am goddamned depressed. You haven't been here as you promised. Where the hell are you?"

First steps with physical therapists at
HealthSouth, Sarasota, Florida.

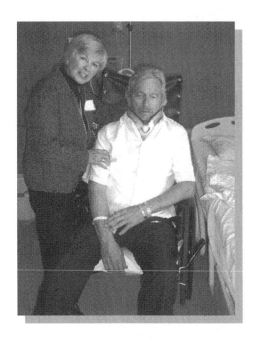

Bill sitting in a wheel chair at Health
South, his eyes still vacant.

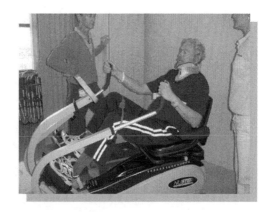

One of Bill's first exercise sessions. He enjoyed
the machine. HealthSouth, Sarasota, Florida.

Dekkers family visiting Bill, April 2009 in Clearwater, Florida.
Clockwise—Alexandra,
Stephanie, Andra, Bill, Marijn, Marina.

Selfie. Left to right—Kathy, Hope, Matthew.

Left to right—Lucca, Rob, Milan.

Hope with her brothers Chas, Art
and John Guzzetta, Cape Coral, Florida, 2009.

Left to right—standing: Alexandra, Andra, Stephanie, Marijn, Marina
(in front of Marijn), Tim, Wendy, Matt, Mathew, Bill, Hope, John, Allison; seated: Samantha, Jacob, Gabriel, Jude.

Saturday, March 21

Another call at 6:23 a.m. at home in Cape Coral. "When in hell are you coming? I might not be here when you arrive. If the military issues orders I'll have to go. No flights have been reserved yet, though. Everything is screwed up as usual."

I am in the middle of the Sunbelt Skyway at 9:00 a.m. on my way to Communicare, when Ronald calls to ask when I will arrive. You are agitated, he says, and have packed your bags again.

When I arrive I try my newly-learned soft voice to help you relax.

"I can't relax! My stomach is on fire! I am so worried!"

My heart aches for you. Doctor Horn says you will remember none of this and I so hope that is true. I know I will remember every godforsaken moment.

The uncertainty of knowing what to expect is very difficult. One moment you are grateful when I have helped you with a word, or a memory, the next you are angry. "Don't patronize me!"

I have no idea what we will face in the months ahead. I pray that your thinking clears. I am convinced that your being here at Communicare is the best place for you right now—as much as you hate it.

When you get discouraged, you tug at my heart strings. Last Monday in the meeting you asked, "What am I being saved for?"

For me, My Dear. For our children and our grandchildren, and friends who love you and want you back. For another 15 to 20 years of life together, please God.

Sunday, March 22

Great way to start the day. You are on a rampage the minute I walk in the door. "Our marriage is over. We are not together anymore at all. We are not a couple. It would take too much counseling to ever get back what we had."

From out in the courtyard I hear someone's iPod playing, "Bridge Over Troubled Waters."

I wonder if we will ever awaken from this nightmare.

Monday, March 23

You were in a good mood when I arrived today. You and Ronald had been over to the cafeteria for breakfast. You offered to come back with me since I hadn't eaten yet. You usually hate going to the cafeteria, but this morning you are Mister Personality.

But when we returned to the apartment you complained about how you hate physical therapy, how demeaning it all is . . .

Before you could get too far down that path, I suggested a trip to Publix. Soon, I wished I had thought of something else.

At Publix you picked up a shish kebob for eight people.

I suggested you put it back.

That made you angry. You then picked up a $30.00 wok and utensils and headed for the checkout.

I sometimes, forgive me God, wish you were back in bed. At least then I had some control.

When we returned, Phong came to work with you.

You chewed her out and refused to do anything she suggested.

You are self-centered and seem to have no feelings for others. You remind me of a self-absorbed teenager. Maybe that is where you are in the rebuilding of yourself.

Ronald suggested we go out for lunch.

You surprised me by accepting.

I sat in the back seat of Ronald's car listening to you regale him with stories of events from our past life. You took what happened two years ago and blended it with something from ten years ago. Some stories you told were total fabrications. But you were so convincing.

We had a wonderful lunch at the Columbia, looking out over the water—for a little while you were happy and life felt like old times.

"Where is my computer?" you shout at me the minute we are back at the apartment.

I explain that it is back in Cape Coral.

"Cape Coral? Why in hell is my laptop in Cape Coral? Is this another one of your tricks? Shit. I'm going for a walk."

When you return you are furious. "Never send Ronald out to follow me again, do you hear me?"

"I didn't send him, Bill. That is his job. His instructions are to always have you in sight."

"Stupid fucking shit."

You sulk through dinner and then tell me it's better if I'm not there. "Get out. Go back to your lavish hotel."

I feel like an open wound tonight and have one of my bend-over rollicking cries.

Tuesday, March 24

We went to Cheddar's for lunch today with Gina. You went to the rest room midway through our meal and returned with a shocked look. "I don't know how I did this, but I seem to have lost my wedding ring.

I checked the towel, but I can't find it."

"Oh, Babe, you haven't worn your ring for almost three months. When you were still in intensive care at Lee Memorial, you were so swollen that I took it off. It's home in a jewelry box."

"Oh, thank goodness. I guess I'm not used to being a wounded soldier."

Back at Communicare, I took my laptop out. I have brought it in today, curious to see how you will handle this. You have been talking about selling stocks and that scares the wits out of me. Our financial advisors are trying to help us, but they advised me that if you call the company that holds our assets, they will have to follow your instructions. Even with a doctor's explanation that you are not capable of making financial decisions now, our advisors maintain that they would have to protect your "rights."

I was just setting up the computer on the kitchen table, when you grabbed it out of my hands and went into the bedroom, placing it on a high chest.

Now, I was mad. "Do not ever grab my computer from me again," I shouted. "This is MY computer and it has everything I am working on, and you WILL NOT destroy all of it"

I reached past you, took the laptop back, and put it into the case. I was so angry I was shaking. I sat on the couch to catch my breath.

After sitting at the kitchen table for a few minutes, you surprised the hell out of me by saying, "You were right. I shouldn't have grabbed it. I won't do it again."

I felt so guilty. Who shouts at her brain-damaged husband?

Later, when I told Doctor Horn about this, he said, "Don't beat up on yourself for being angry with him. I think you brought him back for a few minutes. And he will have to learn to honor some boundaries. I think you handled it fine."

A new caretaker, a young fellow named Chris, came in about 5:00 p.m.

"Where is the nearest BestBuy?" you asked him. I stood behind you, shaking my head no, but Chris didn't seem to get it.

"Oh, not far from here." Chris said. "Just down at the corner of Route 61."

"Okay, let's go," you said to him.

"No, Bill. We are not going down to buy a computer tonight," I said, looking at Chris.

You sent a look of disgust at me. "Chris, will you take me?"

I was astounded when I saw Chris go for the car keys. "Chris, did you not hear me say no?!" "I mean NO."

Finally, the light seemed to dawn and he retired to the bench outside.

Another night of leaving you furious. And tomorrow I leave for Cape Coral.

Wednesday, March 25

I was white-knuckled as usual as I drove the route back to Cape Coral this morning. It is not an easy drive. The first part is over a multi-laned highway until reaching the Skyway Bridge. On the other side of the bridge is another hour of driving on frantic Route 75.

The last time I followed this route I was in a middle lane when I became aware of what seemed to be a travel trailer at a complete stop just ahead. I quickly checked my left mirror, then made a fast switch to the left lane—just in time to fly past a truck pulling a trailer, apparently stalled in the middle of the road. Even though I had a quick thought that—hey!—my reflexes were fast enough to make the correction, my hands were shaking on the steering wheel.

I have to get comfortable with this drive because when you are my passenger I know there will be no room for error. I can just imagine getting off at the wrong exit and trying to find my way back onto the highway. You would blow a gasket.

Before the accident, you always did the driving. We drove from California to Florida and I never took the wheel. It was part of your need to control and I didn't really mind. I enjoyed having the freedom to read or do a crossword puzzle. So in some ways, I guess this has been good for me. Who says an old dog can't learn new tricks? At 70, I am learning to drive on these crazy Florida highways.

Doctor Horn called about 6:00 p.m. You had talked your night caretaker into taking you out to Cheddar's for dinner. While there, you had ordered a beer. The caretaker had said she couldn't stop you without a scene. No one knows what to expect when you have had alcohol, so Doctor Horn said they'd watch you closely tonight.

I joined John, Fran, Chris and Michelle at Applebee's in Cape Coral tonight to celebrate Michelle's 56th birthday. Just as the main course came, my cell phone vibrated. I took it outside.

"I've been thinking about our financial situation. I want to get back on the computer so I can manipulate some stocks. You are keeping important things from me and I don't like it." You hung up.

To bed about 11:00. At 3:30 a.m. you call. "I don't have a schedule. And in case you think I'm getting out of here in a week, it isn't going to happen. They have other plans for me. Just thought you'd want to know." Click. It's hard to get back to sleep.

121

Thursday, March 26

This afternoon, still in Cape Coral, I lay down on the couch, and tried to take a nap, but of course the phone rang.

"Where is my computer? I want to talk to my friends. I feel cut off from the world. I want to order things online."

That gives me the chills.

"And, oh, by the way I am so lucky to have Gina as my caretaker. I still can't make any sense of the calendar, but Gina is in charge here. She is so smart! She remembers things! She is like a mother hen."

Gina is the most attractive of the caretakers and I'm not sure how professional she is. If you are getting a crush on her, I don't know if she will know how to handle it.

I hope my premonition earlier isn't coming true.

Friday, March 27

Rob, Jen and Milan flew into Cape Coral last night. Today they convinced me to hang out by the pool at home with them—the first time I have been near it since the day of our accident.

It was wonderful to have the time with two-year-old-going-on-thirty Milan, who convinced me to get into my swim suit, then promptly pulled me in.

Just a few hours of feeling normal is so refreshing.

Saturday, March 28

Our plan was to drive up this morning in tandem, but Milan got sick during the night, so this morning Rob and Jen took her to a clinic here in Cape Coral. I went on ahead, arriving at Communicare about noon.

You were sitting on the couch and asked me to sit down next to you. "There is probably not a good time to tell you this, but I must. I have taken some of my love for you and have given it to Gina. I have talked to Ronald and to Rotanda about this. I feel very guilty that I have let this happen, but you know, you are not here, and she is always here for me. She comes in the morning and I'm feeling like shit and she tells me how good I'm looking and how much better I am and she cheers me up. We haven't made love, or even touched, but I did tell her how I felt. She got quite angry and said she has a husband and kids and doesn't need this. You and I have lost so much of our marriage that unless I can come home, I don't think we have anything left between us."

I know this is brain damage talking. I must be mature. I must not take this personally.

But my heart is pounding. I saw this coming. I think it could also be blackmail. You want very badly to come home. You might think this will make me want to take you out of here.

I move to sit on the coffee table so I am facing you. "Bill, Gina is your caretaker. She is paid to take care of you. The reason you have to stay here is because you have a whole team of people working with you. It is not uncommon for patients to fall in love with their caretakers. Often pregnant women think they are in love with their obstetricians, who seem to understand their needs so much better than their own husbands. But of course, the doctor is only doing his job, and most likely has a wife and family. Usually, once the patient is no longer in the care of this person, the feelings disappear. So why don't we just . . . let it go?"

You remained morose and distant.

Rob, Jen and Milan arrived about a half an hour later.

"I don't want them to come in," you said. "I am not in the mood for company."

"Well, they have traveled here all the way from California and you are going to see them."

Once they were inside, you seemed delighted to see them.

When we were out in the courtyard later Rob told me that as soon as

I had left the apartment to go out to play with Milan, you had said to them, "I have made a terrible mistake. Don't you ever do it because it'll stay with you for the rest of your life. I've told your mother that I have fallen in love with a Vietnamese girl."

(Gina, whose name you couldn't remember, comes from South America.)

Jennifer told me she had cried, then you had cried, too. "I feel like a big zero, worthless," you'd complained.

I said, "We can't take this seriously."

Rob told me he'd had the presence of mind to say to you, "Bill, this is one I'd get rid of right away. Put that one away."

"Well, this definitely is the Navy's fault," you had told him. "Why would they put a pretty young thing in here to be with a guy who's been in an accident?"

Later, we went to Carrabba's for dinner and you withstood the noise and confusion well.

When we got back to the apartment, Ronald was sitting at your kitchen table sorting out your nighttime meds.

You were furious. "Rob, don't talk to that man! Ronald, you get the fuck out of this room. I told you never to come in here."

Poor Ronald gathered up the meds as fast as he could.

You slammed the door behind him and closed all the blinds.

Back at the motel room I'm alone and blue. Rob, Jen and Milan have left from here for the Caribbean for a little vacation. They begged me to come . . . just for a few days, but I couldn't do it. Just couldn't.

Sometimes the only way I can relieve the throat-tightening stress is to really let 'er rip and have a great hysterical cry in my hotel room. Punch the pillows, kick the bed. Finally, that lump in my throat disappears. After a glass of wine I can usually sleep.

Crying seems to relieve your tension as well; I notice that after crying you are often more lucid.

We have had good news from our lawyer. He has found insurance payments that are due to us that I never would have thought to look for. These payments will pay for your stay at Communicare! Thank goodness I hired a lawyer to help us through this.

There are signs that your short-term memory is beginning to return. Earlier today I brought in pictures of our house in Cape Coral and when

I showed them to you, you smiled, nodded and asked why there was a sign for a security company on the front lawn. Art had installed a security system after your hospitalization, knowing how I do not like staying alone, and fearing that I would have many nights alone there.

I'd been elated. "Wow, Bill, you haven't been able to remember our house in Cape Coral for months. And you are right. That sign was not there before the accident. Wow! This is huge."

You burst into tears.

Sunday, March 29

It is now a little over three months since the accident. Was life ever just normal? When it was, I would wish for . . . oh, a luxurious trip, a vacation at a beach. But now I just long to go back to normal. Just give me day-in-day-out, breakfast, lunch and dinner, with a husband whose brain is working and with whom I can share life again. After what we've been through, it would be enough! Hell, it would be heaven.

You have been so agitated lately that several days ago I called Doctor Horn at home. He called Doctor Tanner, who upped your Seroquel dose. I thought that would elevate your mood, but you continued in a funk.

"You know, you are wearing me down," I said.

"I'm wearing myself down," you responded.

You can't stop talking about Ronald, calling him an asshole, a jerk. He is still on duty as your weekend caretaker, but no more interesting trips, no more lunches at the beach. He now spends all of his time sitting on the bench outside your apartment.

I think I can sense what's bothering you about Ronald. He really wants to be helpful and he is kind. But without realizing it, he has been too much in your space, sometimes overbearing. He enjoyed the "talks" the two of you had in the evening after I left in the early days of his caretaking. But even then I sensed that sometimes it was too anxiety-producing for you.

Often when I left, I would say, "Please remember, Ronald, from now until bedtime, no controversial discussions. Just speak softly to him, okay?"

He always agreed, but I don't think it was in him. He is just naturally loud and outgoing, and I think that was too much stimulation for you. You didn't know how to analyze that, so you just decided you hated him.

Even with your propensity to be nasty to caretakers, you are a star here. Most others are in much worse shape than you. Here you are, this tall, good looking, white-haired guy, out walking the path at 6:00 a.m. when everyone else is still sleeping. And you can still carry on an intelligent conversation, especially about issues that occurred well before the accident.

I think you have convinced most of the helpers you are richer than God, as you talk about your "accountants" and make remarks, like "We're wealthy. We can do whatever we want to do."

You and I decided that we would go out for dinner alone tonight. You looked in the yellow pages to find someplace "interesting."

I reminded you that driving after dark is out for me. "There are some good restaurants right nearby that we can manage fine," I said.

But you were adamant you would find someplace new and that I would drive.

Finally, I said, "Look, here are the choices—"

You slammed your hand down on the coffee table. "You see? Everything I used to decide you have taken over. I feel like a complete zero. I have no control over my life anymore. I have no base. I don't think you and I will ever be able to salvage anything. Too much has been lost. You keep saying everything will be all right, but I don't think so. I think the Bill you once knew won't be back. Someone with a brain injury like mine will probably never be the same. You may be waiting for a bus that never comes into the station."

Your words hit me like pellets of sleet on bare skin. And I fear you may be right. This is the first time I have let this in.

We had dinner at Carrabba's where you continued to pout. "What's food without wine?"

Later, back at the apartment, while you took a shower I changed your sheets. When you emerged from the shower, I said to you, "Here's what I think is dangerous. You have made me out to be the bad guy. I have been thrust into this role. I have to make decisions. But I'll tell you what. I am not the bad guy. I CAN drink, but I choose not to when I am with you. And I don't continuously bitch about it."

You looked chagrined. "I deserved that. I'm glad you said it."

You looked so sad as I prepared to leave.

I kissed you good night and said, "Look, you have clean sheets and clean pajamas. I know you wish for more and there will be. We have to be patient."

You shrugged, looking out the window, and simply said, "Yeah."

Monday, March 30

When I arrived, I was surprised to find Gina still on duty with you this morning. A note was on the apartment door saying you were at the cafeteria. Sure enough, you and Gina were having a bagel. Gina is wearing a low cut top, exposing décolleté. How damned unfair. You are so vulnerable right now and so is our marriage. We should be protected from this. The administration should have replaced her with someone else, or at least insisted she cover herself.

Later you told me that you and Gina had had a conversation about your feelings for her, and that you'd told me.

She'd asked how I felt and you told her that you thought I was hurt, but I'd be ok. "I want you to know that I am grateful that I could share my feelings with you and you didn't get angry. I thought about what Rob said . . . that I should walk away from this . . . and I think that's what I should do. I think I'm back on track now. Besides, I don't think she wants me anyway. She has a husband of her own."

You look like a mature, dignified, businessman and you talk like a high school freshman. But . . . maybe this is progress.

In our weekly meeting, the staff agreed that Gina should be phased out as your caretaker and Renee will move in to take her place.

Tuesday, March 31

Gina and Renee were in your room when I arrived back on campus. "He's been waiting for you!" they chirped. You seemed very happy to see me.

We left immediately for lunch at Cheddar's where as soon as we were seated, you said you had things you had to get off your chest. How much more of this can I take?

"I fear I made a big mistake by letting my emotions get away from me."

"It's all right, Bill. It's a thing of the past. Over."

Then you lean in close and say, "I have a question to ask you. Are you leaving me here at night because you have found someone else?"

"Are you kidding? No way."

"I didn't know," you said. "I've been trying to imagine what you do when you leave here and suddenly I thought you were seeing someone else—someone waiting for you at the hotel."

Later that afternoon Brian arrived noisily, as he does three times a week, on his Harley, the braid down his back peeking out from under his helmet. He is an excellent, talented speech therapist. Today he challenged you with some deductive reasoning exercises. You seemed to realize for the first time you aren't thinking as clearly as you once did. You knew there would have been a time when you could have figured the puzzle out easily. You did not react with anger this time, but with wistfulness.

Taking up your pencil, you turned to Brian. "This is how I feel," you said. You drew a large circle with "world" written inside it. Next to it, but not touching, was a much smaller circle. Inside that one, you wrote, "Me." "I keep trying to get 'me' into the 'world', but I can't quite make it."

It makes me sad, but delights Brian. "That is really good, Bill! You have found a great way to illustrate how you feel."

After your session with Brian you went into the bedroom for a nap. I lay down on the couch, trying to rest a few minutes, but you were up in about twenty minutes. You were surprised to see me. "How long have you been here?"

"All day."

"All day? It's morning. You must have gotten here before I woke up."

"No, Bill, it is afternoon. Remember this morning we went grocery shopping and then to Office Max to buy you a calendar?"

"That feels like yesterday." You sat down on the couch next to me and shook your head. "I can't trust anything."

I took your hand in mine. "That must be hard as hell. Here's what has happened. We had an accident and you were taken to Lee Memorial Hospital. Then later you were transferred to HealthSouth. Now you are at Communicare, another rehabilitation facility."

You shook your head. "I don't remember any of it. I don't know where the hell I am."

We have a new caretaker who agreed to take us to a restaurant in Tampa for dinner. She drove us there, then picked us up later. That way we didn't have to worry about it getting dark before our return. Perfect.

Once we were seated, you complained about not having wine. "Look around you," I told you. "A lot of people enjoy dinner without wine. We don't dare take even a tiny chance of creating a problem in your brain's healing process.

"John and Jeanne are coming to visit tomorrow," I told you, hoping to change the focus.

"Do we have a barbecue at home in Cape Coral?"

"Yes."

"Then, why can't we take John and Jeanne home? We'll barbecue. We could spend the night there and come back in the morning!"

"Um . . . I think it's too late to let John and Jeanne know about the change. Maybe next time . . ." To my surprise, you accepted that answer.

Later I put my arms around you as I prepared to leave. You rested your chin on the top of my head and said, "I wish we were shacking up tonight."

Wednesday, April 1

7:15 a.m. Ah, yes, my morning call. I reach for my cell.

"I've been awake all night. The caretakers all gathered outside my room and they were very noisy. I need a ride someplace this morning, but I'm not sure where. I already called Ben and told him I needed a ride, but if you're coming soon, I'll call him back and tell him that you'll take me."

You have called Ben many times during the night and he always takes your call and, usually, calms you down. This seems to go well beyond what a staff member is required to do.

When I arrived, Jason, a new caretaker, was with you in your apartment. He came out to greet me. When he turned to re-enter the apartment, you said, "Okay, you're free to go now. Out! Get out!"

John and Jeanne arrived about 11:15. It had been raining all morning and was still dark and gloomy. John had designed a clever graph to show you how far you have progressed. He's hoping to help you understand why it is important for you to stay here and continue working with the therapists. At one end of the graph, at the bottom of the page, he'd written "December 27. The accident. Inability to talk, walk or breathe on your own." The line went up to the date that your trach was removed, then up to your transfer to HealthSouth. Further up, he'd labeled the day you first walked, etc. The line went almost to the top, but left the last few spaces vacant, obviously waiting to be filled in. You looked at the chart, but didn't comment. I pinned it to your bulletin board, hoping you'd study it later. Jeanne brought out a tin of her fabulous chocolate chip cookies.

You were determined that we would return to Island View for lunch, but all they were serving was a brunch at $25 a head, which was fine with you, the great spender, but the rest of us voted for something closer and less expensive. We ended up at Cheddar's.

You seemed delighted to be with friends and ordered ribs, catfish, and several sides. As usual, you ate only half or less of the food on your plate. We talked about next summer's social activities at the yacht club. Looking forward to that cheered us all up. I hated to see them leave, but they wanted to get back before the heavy 5:00 p.m. traffic.

We spent the rest of the afternoon sitting in the courtyard on the swing, each of us reading a book. At five, I went over to bring back our dinners from the cafeteria. We went inside to eat at the coffee table, where we could continue reading. When I stacked all the dishes on the tray to return to the cafeteria, you looked up at me and said, "You know, being here so quietly and normally with you has made this the happiest day I have ever had here." We embraced and held one another for a few minutes.

You walked me to the car. "You made me feel special today," you said. "Thank you."

I was awakened during the night to a loud clap of thunder. This thought popped into my mind: Maybe we have been given a gift—to help us appreciate the simple act of being together and being healthy.

I love you very much, especially when you are so vulnerable. All of my maternal, protective feelings are firing. I hope we both sleep well tonight and that we can soon do that together.

Thursday, April 2

You have an appointment with Doctor Mayer in Sarasota this morning. Rotanda will drive, but I needed to be at the facility by 6:45. I forgot that it would still be dark at that hour. Even the short drive from the hotel was difficult. With these damned cataracts, all the lights have haloes around them. The haloes blend together, covering up what is in between. When I turned onto the exit, I almost back ended a car at the end of the ramp waiting to turn.

I parked in my usual spot under the trees across from the apartment and when I looked up I could see into the apartment through your open blinds. You were silhouetted and, Oh God, I knew what you were doing. Packing again.

I was barely in the door when you barked, "Where is my fucking small bag? I need it to pack my pajamas in."

The night caretaker quickly took a powder, saying, "I'll give you two some privacy." I think she was scared. Who's to blame her?

I explained to you we were not staying overnight and that you didn't need to pack your pajamas, but you were sure that I was lying, somehow trying to subvert you. When Rotanda arrived, you asked her, "Don't I have to pack my bag for this?"

She just shook her head. "Uh-uh."

You looked confused. I can't even imagine how hard this must be for you. You have wildly firing neurons in your brain giving you false, or only partially correct messages. How long will it take to clear? In some ways, the more it clears, the harder it becomes because you are beginning to recognize your deficiencies, and that leads to great frustration and sadness for you.

As we left, Renee was crossing the courtyard, preparing to check in for work. She gave you a hug and wished you well.

We had thought you would have an x-ray at 9:00 a.m., followed immediately by your appointment with Doctor Mayer, but the receptionist informed us you weren't scheduled to see the doctor until 11:00 a.m. So we had an hour and a half wait. Sometimes I want to yell at innocent people, "Don't you know that he has been brain damaged?! Don't you understand that waiting around for an hour and a half is going to be very difficult?" They don't because you look perfectly normal.

Rotanda found a parking spot outside the medical arts building where your doctor's appointment was scheduled. We'd all brought books, so she suggested we settle back and read. It was a beautiful day. We opened all the windows to let the breeze in and I thought—this will be all right.

It lasted five minutes. "I'm hungry," you said. "I'll wait here and you two go get me something to eat from the restaurant over there."

"We can't leave you alone, Bill," I said.

"Rotanda, then drive me through Taco Bell."

"It's against the rules to eat in the company car," she said.

Fact is we were both worried about losing our perfect parking spot and having to walk a long distance back to the medical arts building. We are never sure when you are going to say that you're tired and don't want to go any further.

Suddenly, you threw open your door and leapt out of the car. Pointing your finger at me, as I tried to climb out of the back seat, you yelled, "I'm going to walk over to Taco Bell and get something to eat. You stay here. I don't want you near me!"

You walked fast across the busy parking lot, unaware of moving cars.

I caught up to you. "You are behaving inappropriately. You are being rude!"

You continued to stomp on, entered Taco Bell and ordered two tacos, took them and sat at a table.

Rotanda and I sat at a nearby table. "How cute do you think he is now?" I asked Rotanda.

"Not very."

When you finished your tacos, you stomped out and headed back toward the car, with us in pursuit. These days are exhausting.

The doctor's appointment was all good news. Your C scan showed all fluids had been absorbed. But the best news was that you could remove your neck brace you have had to wear 24/7 since the accident because of your broken neck. You have been a great sport about wearing it, until just lately when it began to bother you. We are ecstatic to not have to worry about that anymore.

On the way home I suggested that we have lunch at the Bonefish Grill. You were very pleased with the choice—a restaurant with white tablecloths and an extensive seafood menu. You were in a good mood until I ordered quiche.

"Quiche!" you bellowed. "Quiche at a seafood restaurant? You are embarrassing yourself and me."

I had reached my limit for this day. "Listen, it is my damned lunch and I will order whatever I choose to order. It is none of your damned business and don't try to pull that know-it-all stuff with me anymore."

That seemed to sober you and the rest of the meal was pleasant.

On the way back to Communicare, you said, "I should apologize for my actions this morning."

"Wow," I said. "Bill, that is a good thing you are saying. It means that you remembered how you behaved and that you felt some remorse for hurting our feelings. That is real growth!"

"Thanks," you said sheepishly.

I asked Rotanda to exit the highway and drive through the mall near Sarasota.

"This is ringing a bell," you said. It was exactly what I'd hoped for. "Didn't we meet Peter and Joette here for lunch? We drove around in here just like this and you called them on your cell phone."

"Yes! We were on our way to Cape Coral, from up North, only a little over a week before the accident, and we called them to meet us for lunch. That you remember something so close to the accident is great! It's coming back, my friend!"

"Yeah, I think I'm getting better. I'm not stumbling over facts so much."

My heart is bursting with joy. There is hope, and it dawns more every day. Thank you, God.

Speaking of thanking God, I have been posting on CaringBridge every night and I am amazed at the huge response we have had from friends. There have been several thousand messages for us. This outpouring of caring from our friends and colleagues has been powerful.

Friday, April 3

You have been working on a computer with one of your caretakers at the main building, and my latest great concern, shared by your doctors, is that you can get into our finances online, and in your present state, that could be a disaster for us. The other day Doctor Horn and Ron Steele advised me to seek a guardianship. "I don't think you have a choice," said Ron.

"What the hell is a guardianship?"

"You go to court and explain that your husband isn't capable at this time of making financial and other decisions and ask the court to make you his guardian. That way you have control over everything."

Oh, brother. What will this do to our marriage? I wonder if you will ever forgive me. I'm not sure this is the right thing to do.

The next day I had just returned to Cape Coral when you called. You told me you had called the credit union and told them that your credit card was lost and you ordered a new one to be FedExed to you immediately.

I called the credit union and explained the problem. The representative explained that they could block the order this one time, but that if you ordered again they could not stop it. It would violate your rights.

Yesterday you yelled at me, "Why am I being kept on such a short leash concerning money. Do you think I have lost my mind?"

Sunday, April 5

I gathered up the garbage in the apartment this morning and was opening the front door to take it to the car so I could transport it to the garbage area.

"I'll take it to the dumpster," you said. "Where are the keys?"

"No, I don't think it's a good idea for you to drive, even here on campus. I'll take it over."

"I SAID I want the keys."

"No, Bill, it is not allowed."

Your eyes were blazing. "I can't believe you are going to stand pat on that!" You slammed out the door and sat on the chair, fuming.

After I delivered the garbage, I came into the apartment and sat on the couch, reading the Sunday paper. You came in, picked up your notebook, and sat down at the kitchen table. In a few minutes, you turned in your chair and faced me. "Are you going to ask what I've been writing?"

"Sure, I've been curious."

"Well, here, read the fucking thing. I am writing about why all of my privileges have been taken away."

Pacing now, voice rising.

"Why am I being punished? I have no money. No computer. I am cut off from my children, my friends. I think I will never get out of here. And you're in that control circle. You won't help me! You don't care! You have all of your freedoms—to drive, to stay at your posh hotel, to go back to Cape Coral. Why don't you just admit it? You don't give a shit about me. You don't care!"

"Don't care?! For the last three months my entire life has been you! I have been thinking of nothing else. I have supported you, taken care of you . . ."

I walked out, stomped around the campus, breathing hard, wanting to punch something. Gradually I calmed down. Who can blame you for feeling lost? You don't understand what has happened.

I returned to the apartment. "I'm sorry I blew up."

You looked innocent, confused. "I'm sorry you had to blow up. I just don't understand. Can you explain?"

"Yes. Your brain has been damaged. It is healing, but you cannot see your own progress, or understand your own disability. This is why you can't drive. We aren't certain that you could handle any situation that arose. Would you panic if someone pulled out in front of you? Would you accidentally step on the accelerator instead of the brake? You still aren't that steady on your feet. There are tests you can take in a short time that will give us these answers. But I can't let you drive before then."

"OK. I guess sometimes I go off on a tangent, but I am so god-damned lonely and I just can't understand why all of my privileges…

"Do you want to go out for lunch today?"

"No, I don't feel like it."

"OK. You have a choice. You can waste today in a blue funk. Or we can have a wonderful, fun day. Art and Di are coming over and we can go to the Columbia for lunch. Your call."

You pace. Finally, "OK, I'll try. I want to have a good day."

"Let's take our books and go to the hotel and sit by the pool until Art and Di get here."

"I forgot we planned to do that. Great!"

Lounging in your chair by the pool, you reach over and take my hand. "I wish we could do this for about four days."

"We will, my love. We will."

"I want to thank you for talking me through this." Tears stream down your cheeks. I get up to put my arms around you. God give me the strength to continue holding you up.

Then, as if a new page has been turned, you reach for your backpack. "I brought my new phone book. I think I'll start putting the new names in it." After a few minutes, you push the books away. "I can't do this. I can't concentrate. I'm making too many mistakes. When in the hell will this be over?"

Monday, April 6

You called several times during the night. At 6:20 a.m. your call centered on your speech. "Are you going to be here in time to do the intro?" Another call at 6:40. "Where is Tim? Home? What the fuck is he doing at home? Who will make the fucking introductions?"

When I arrived you stood up from the kitchen table and came to greet me. "Why aren't you leveling with me? Do you know that I have to beg for money to just buy a loaf of bread or a bag of cookies? I feel totally emasculated. Why can't I have a credit card? Why are you punishing me? I don't want you around me. Get out of here."

I picked up my purse and walked out the door.

You rushed to the door and shouted, "Don't leave!"

I kept walking through the courtyard.

Gina and Renee walked toward me. "You have to understand," Gina said sweetly. "He is a man who has always been in control. This is very hard on him"

Like I didn't realize that? I wanted to shout, "Shut up! He is my husband and how dare you 'explain' him to me?" I knew that it was time for me to set limits on these outbursts. Brain injured or not, I still know you better than anyone else. I stomped around the campus until I could settle down, then returned to sit on the swing.

Renee had gone into your room and was in there for over half an hour. She emerged and approached me. "He wants to apologize."

I wanted to say, "Fine, let him come out and do it," but I gave in.

You were sitting on the couch, your head hung low. "I'm sorry, but I feel so punished."

Word of this confrontation spread quickly to staff. Shortly Ben came ambling over. "Look, I have an idea. Why not open a credit card for Bill at the local bank, but we'll put a limit on it. That way he can go to the grocery store and pay for his purchases in a way that seems normal, but he would be held to a budget." I didn't think you'd go for it, but you did.

I called our financial advisor and we have set up a time for him to call you today. He agreed to discuss our investments with you to the extent you could understand. We hope you will feel like you are regaining control over your life.

At 11:30 a.m., exactly on time, the phone rang. Placing my hand over the mouthpiece, I said to you, "Remember we have a financial planning meeting today. Here is Bill Burns." I handed the phone to you.

After a moment of you listening, I heard you say, "Fine. Just fine, if you like hanging out with brain damaged people this is the place to be."

Then, "Maybe you think that's funny, but I don't! I don't like being laughed at." You angrily tossed the phone back to me.

Poor Bill Burns was stricken. "Did I say something wrong? I am so sorry. I thought that remark was the old dry humor we always knew Bill for. I never meant to hurt his feelings!"

"It's okay," I told him. "These days we never know what to expect."

Mid- afternoon, Ben came by to pick us up to go to the bank to sign up for your new credit card. You seemed poised filling out the paperwork and got your name and address down without a problem. When you reached the line asking for the date, you stopped and raised one eyebrow. "April 6, 2009," I whispered.

We had dinner in your apartment, sent over from the cafeteria, sitting side by side on the couch. You talked about how much you miss sleeping together, sharing our life. "I am so lonely." You put your head in your hands and cried. I put my arms around you and we cried together, rocking back and forth. Drying our tears, we agreed that when this thing is over, we are going on a long, wonderful trip.

Tuesday, April 7

You are nonplussed, but slightly amused at yourself this morning. You had been awake most of the night worrying about getting ready for your dentist's appointment. You had showered and were sitting on the couch waiting for it to turn light, when it dawned on you that the appointment isn't until tomorrow. This seems to be a huge step. Several steps. You got yourself ready. You knew you had a dentist's appointment. You realized that it wasn't until the next day.

Even though you'd had little sleep, you wanted to do something "interesting." Roger suggested the aquarium. Carrie, your caretaker for the day, agreed to drive us there. A dolphin show began shortly after our arrival, accompanied by horrendously loud music and a female commentator with a piercing voice. I cringed when I heard it, knowing it would be more than your nervous system could handle. But you were gracious. "You and Carrie stay and watch the show," you said. "I'm going outside and sit on the bench. I can't stand another minute of that screaming woman."

Later at the Columbia for lunch you tried to order wine, but accepted my admonition. You were in a great mood. Just get you to a waterside table in a good seafood restaurant and you're happy.

Back on campus, we settled in on the swing in the courtyard with our books. After a few minutes, you said, "Let's go someplace."

"We just returned."

"I know, but I want to get out of this hellhole. Maybe you like it here, but I don't. Of course, you stay in a luxurious hotel."

I took my book and moved to the picnic table. I am very tired of this. I was not prepared for so much that has happened. Your deep loneliness is heartbreaking. I didn't foresee your frustration at not having money or that you would blame me for all of this. Naively, I thought that your abilities would keep pace with your desires.

This damn hard headedness of yours, your determination, is probably what will pull you through this, but it scares me that when you want something, you want it now and you think the only thing between what you want and where you are, is me.

It got hot at the picnic bench, so I went into the apartment where you had gone to take a nap. I lay down on the couch. In about fifteen minutes you emerged from the bedroom. "Oh, are you still here? I had a dream that you were pissed off because I was taking a nap and left. I am getting sick of these vivid dreams!"

You knew it was a dream!

You sat down next to me on the couch. "Help me understand why I have to stay here. I'm afraid nobody ever gets out of here. How can I escape this prison? Does word have to come from you? Listen. Send Amo Houghton (*our Congressman*) $1,000 and tell him I want out."

I explained again, "It is important for you to be here while your wound is still 'fresh.' That's the most important time for new connections to be made in your brain. You have already made great progress, but if we go home too soon you will miss the opportunity to get as well as possible. Doctor Horn has seen this happen. People think they are all right, but when they get home they discover that they still can't do things that used to be easy for them. They get more and more frustrated. Please, let's just stay the course here. Get the most out of it we can. And by the way, here's an example of why you need to keep working. You stumbled and almost fell twice during physical therapy outside this morning. Phong had to catch you. You scared the wits out of me."

"Me, too," you admitted. "Can we go out for dinner?"

After dinner, we went to the hotel and sat by the pool. You love doing this. I think it makes you forget that you are a patient. You told me how happy you are that I am keeping a journal. "I think if you read some Grisham," you told me, "it would be helpful for you. He is so skilled at rounding out characters." You agreed that it would be helpful if you wrote down your feelings.

Back at Communicare we got out of the car, but instead of heading for your apartment, you said, "I guess I'll take a little walk around the grounds before turning in. You should get on the road, though, before it's totally dark. You leaned over and kissed me goodnight."

"You remind me of the old Bill Moffett tonight."

"Really? I wasn't aware that the old Bill Moffett was gone."

I am realizing that the times during which you are lucid are outnumbering the times you are still confused. It is not a straight line, but I think we're winning.

Wednesday, April 8

Today you can't stop talking about sex. "The docs are just trying to keep us apart to exert control. I'm sick of it. They won't let you stay in my room with me. They are just jerking us around."

Doctor Tanner has explained to me that this is not unusual, especially with male patients. "They think they're going to be very great in bed, but usually they can't perform. This is a very tricky area." Don't I know it?

Doctor Horn thinks you must realize that you still have deficits. In the staff meeting today, he showed you your scores in a recent test, that illustrated how, when you tire, your scores plummet. Before the meeting, you were already sad because you are still having problems understanding a calendar. Somehow you just can't grasp the concept of each day having a designation, a month, a day of the month, and that one follows after the other. When your caretaker asks what day it is, you stare at the calendar, shake your head, and look sad. "I just don't get it."

Thursday, April 9

This is a day I have dreaded, but knew must come. Today is my appointment with Lance McKinney, a lawyer in Fort Myers specializing in elder issues. Thank goodness, Chas came in yesterday.

The receptionist ushered us into a conference room where Chas and I were seated on one side of a long table. Soon Lance appeared. He is a young (forties) dark haired spare man, with a warm and hearty handshake. He reminds me of the televangelist, Joel Osteen.

I explained to him about our accident, your traumatic brain injury, and the advice of all of your caretakers and our financial planners. He listened carefully, although he'd probably heard this story hundreds of times.

"I think there is no question that this is the right thing to do," he said. "And I think you are wise to do it now. I had a case last year where the wife of a lawyer came to me two years after he had suffered TBI. He'd been released from treatment and appeared to friends to be normal again. But what only she knew was that he was making very poor decisions concerning money. She was concerned that he would bankrupt them. When she filed, he became infuriated and they ended up divorcing.

It was hard to hold back tears as I listed our assets, making this huge step seem very real. You already feel emasculated and controlled. Wait until you hear what I did today!

McKinney explained that an attorney would be appointed to represent you. He or she will visit you and explain the process and also observe your level of acuity. This is intended to protect your rights.

At the conclusion of our meeting, the lawyer accompanied me out into the waiting room where Chas was waiting. As they shook hands, he said to Chas, "Does she have a support system?"

"Yes, we are a large family and we are all committed to helping Hope and Bill through this terrible time."

"It is a good thing. She is going to need it," said McKinney.

Good Friday, April 10

When Chas and I arrived at the campus this morning, you were returning from Publix with Renee. You had bought an Easter lily for me and had three other bouquets.

"This lily is beautiful," I said to you. "Who are the other bouquets for?"

"The girls," you said. "I wanted something for them when they arrive later today."

"I hate to tell you this, my Dear, but the girls are back in Boston. They aren't planning a trip here today."

You heaved a great sigh and shook your head. "Goddamn," you said under your breath.

Chas tagged along behind as we went into the apartment where you ignored him. When I told you two weeks ago that Chas was coming, you were not happy. But everything is changing so rapidly I thought you'd be in a very different place by now. I realize you are sensing your own lack of acuity, and maybe you are embarrassed to have him see you like that. You have corresponded with one another for years, and have enjoyed one another's razor sharp sense of humor. I think you know at some level you can't compete in your present condition and it embarrasses you. I wish I wasn't putting either of you through this. But, damn, I so looked forward to having him here. He stood, gazing out the window, hands behind his back, probably thinking this would be a long three days.

Chas had suggested that we might have a meeting with Doctor Horn while he was here. At the age of almost 80, he still teaches at Hunter College. At about 2:00 p.m. Doctor Horn came to the apartment and soon Ben Pulcher arrived. And actually, it was you who asked good questions.

What about driving? Alcohol Consumption? When could you sleep with your wife again?

To which the answers were: driving only after a special exam developed especially for patients with TBI was administered and it was determined that you were safe to do so. Doctor Horn thought alcohol consumption would never be a good idea, an answer you didn't want to hear. You didn't notice he didn't answer the third question.

You had loosened up with Chas over lunch. After the meeting was over and we were alone in the apartment, you told Chas there was a caretaker named Gina who had told you she had gallstones and couldn't

146

afford an operation. You wanted to help her out financially, you said.

Chas said, "Bill, Gina should not have discussed this situation with you. You are not the person who should be helping her."

"But she doesn't have any insurance," you insisted. "I want to go to the administration here and tell them that they can't just leave her out to dry here. She has to have some help."

You were getting worked up over this, but Chas talked quietly to you about why this is a situation you should leave to others. You looked as if you were trying to take in what he was saying, scowling in concentration, nodding.

When it was time for us to go that evening, you said, "You don't have to hurry back in the morning. I'll be all right." This sounded great, because you usually are spiteful when I leave. It felt good to leave on a positive note.

Saturday, April 11

My phone rang at 6:00 a.m. "Where are you? I got up and looked for your things and couldn't find them. So I took a shower and thought maybe you'd be in bed when I finished, but you were not. Why aren't you here?

I explained once again that I was at the hotel.

"Please, I need you. I don't know what the fuck is going on."

"Remember. Yesterday Chas and I spent the day with you. We had lunch together.

"That was four days ago! Goddamn, when will this dreaming stop?"

"Look, I'll be there in about an hour. Why don't you go over to the cafeteria and get some breakfast. By the time you finish, I'll probably be there.

"Is Chas coming with you?"

"Yes."

"Oh, fuck!"

Chas and I skipped breakfast at the hotel to get to you as fast as we could. You were agitated, and had not gone for breakfast. You stared at Chas, but refused to acknowledge him, so he went outside and sat on the chair in the courtyard, while I prepared breakfast. When he joined us at the breakfast table you were barely civil.

After I'd cleaned up, we all went to the hotel where you have always enjoyed sitting at a table by the pool.

The three of us seated ourselves around the table with an umbrella. You turned to me. "I don't want your brother sitting at the same table with us." Chas took his book and moved to another table. Oh God, how I wish I had waived him off. I know that you need me and that you are not thinking clearly. But Chas has been such a huge support and doesn't deserve to be treated like this. This is definitely one of the worst weekends of my life.

In a few minutes, you said you wanted to take a nap and you wanted me to come with you. I climbed in next to you and put my arm over you. You were unyielding, then said, "Stop that! Your brother can walk in here and discover us at any moment!"

"Okay. I think I'll go outside and read while you sleep."

When I returned to the room you said, "Oh, you did come back. I didn't think you would. Come sit here next to me, will you? You know I thought this would all be different. I thought I would be so glad to be with you that all of our past together would rush in, everything we've worked for, all the love we had would come back to me."

"How do you feel?" I asked.

"Empty. You know, when I tell the people at Communicare about all we have done together, they are impressed. They want to hear more. They think we're perfect," you said softly.

"Well, we have had a wonderful life. And we will have a normal life again. Just a few more weeks."

You really have been improving on all fronts. Your walks with Phong have made you strong and agile. You are now allowed to walk off campus. You enjoy strolling through the neighborhoods surrounding Communicare. Brian, your speech therapist, is delighted with the improvement in your deductive reasoning skills. At the weekly meetings, everyone who works with you remarks on how amazed they have been at your improvement, especially for someone 70 years old.

Others at the facility don't seem to progress. Many of them will spend the rest of their days as patients. Lonnie is two doors down, just on the other side of the laundry room. She is bent over in her wheel chair, her blond hair streaming over her cheeks as she pushes herself along with her legs, apparently her strongest limbs. When she looks up, and the hair falls away, she stuns you with her smile. She gazes out at the surroundings, straining to keep her head up. "I used to climb trees," she says wistfully. Often we hear blaring rock music coming from her apartment. I wonder if that helps her escape her demons.

Kevin used to be a construction worker until he got in the way of a semi, is how Ben describes his plight. He is always shouting, pushing himself furiously forward, his feet clad in rubber storm boots. "They've got my goddamned insurance money. Why in the hell can't they do it right?" He has to be fed liquid food, served in a bucket from which he spoons, spilling a good share of the food on its way to his mouth.

Melissa has been here over a year. She had a scholarship to Harvard before she had her accident. She, too, suffered severe TBI and other injuries that have left her with a limp and a mind that doesn't operate like it once did. The staff recently rented her an apartment in town where she will soon live on her own. But, they are moving her there gradually. At first, she is allowed a few hours. Then a full day. Finally, they allowed her to spend the entire weekend in her new apartment. She was in seventh heaven. Within weeks she's scheduled to be permanently moved. Still, she will be looked in on periodically, and will continue rehabilitation exercises. There is no way of knowing if she could ever move out completely on her own.

You do not care to be near these people. I think they scare you and that you do not want to be identified with them.

Easter Sunday, April 12

You, Chas and I went to the Columbia for lunch. Thank God, you were courteous, if not warm, to Chas. You explained to him that your caretakers say you are about on schedule with your recovery. We had a pleasant chat over fresh fish and enjoyed the warm breeze coming off the bay.

Back at the campus, Chas asked you if you would show him around the grounds. "I'd like to see where you walk," he said, "So I can describe it to Nancy when I get home."

You seemed delighted and walked him around both the inside and outside tracks. "The older caretakers can't keep up with me," you told him proudly. "They have to send the younger ones."

Then the three of us sat out in the courtyard. Chas told you that he'd be leaving in the morning.

"I want to tell you about one of my caretakers," you told him. "She is such a great woman. She really cares about me—the real me. I am convinced that the love of these people who have worked with me had a huge effect on my recovery."

"That's great Bill," Chas said. "It is wonderful to have good caretakers. But the fact is they are being paid for it."

"That's not fair! That cheapens the whole thing. These people really care—and not just because they're being paid. Oh, and I am grateful to your sister, too, because she found this facility. I'd be a vegetable like some of these other people if it wasn't for her."

"You'd be dead if it weren't for her," Chas said quietly.

Then you went over and sat next to him. "Sorry if I was preoccupied while you were here. I want you to know that I appreciate your coming here and I am realizing why I am getting better. I look at these people and say, "There but for the grace of God . . . Your sister, my wife . . ."" You just hung your head. Chas patted you on the back and we got up to leave.

As we pulled away to return to the hotel, I glanced in the rearview mirror. You had returned to the swing where several caretakers had gathered around you. You appeared to be holding court.

Tuesday, April 14

This is the day I usually return to Cape Coral, and I had planned that, but the weather was daunting. Forecasters were reporting tornado warnings. The sky, that had been clear when I awoke, turned black while I had breakfast. By 9:00 a.m. it was pouring. I checked with Peter and Joette Knott, who live in Bradenton, about halfway between Clearwater and Cape Coral, and Peter advised me to stay put. The weather there was severe, he said. So I called you and said, "Do you want some company today? I don't think I dare drive in this weather." You seemed happy.

Doctor Galloway, the founder of Communicare, was on campus today and when he heard that we were together in the apartment he came over. A large man, with a booming voice, he's proud of his Irish heritage.

You and I sat on the couch. He pulled a kitchen chair over to face us. "It's good to see you, Friend," he bellowed to you. "We are very proud of the headway you have made while you were here. But there is something I want to tell you. You know, the victim of the brain injury is not the only victim. Loved ones take a lot of verbal abuse and they become victims, too. Many families simply can't take it and leave the patients for us to take care of. But the residents who have strong family support recuperate faster and to a much larger degree," he said.

"Well I know how much this gal has done," you said bending your head toward me.

"Well by Golly, this IS growth, My Friend," he roared. "A couple of weeks ago you wanted to kick her ass out of here and get a divorce."

"I did?" you said. "Oh, no! I'm sure glad you didn't take me up on it."

Doctor Galloway stayed a few more minutes, complimenting you on your headway. I like the man very much.

The sky darkened even more and the rain came down in torrents. I wouldn't be leaving today.

You had scheduled a meeting this afternoon with your psychologist, John Gallagher, so I went along. "We're losing our professional status," you told John. "We were icons. I hate to give that up."

"I know how hard it is to be patient," John said. "But your injury is really 'fresh' as far as brain injuries go. You have made an amazing recovery, and I believe that will continue. It has only been months."

"It's a good thing I've had the Navy," you said.

I put my hand on your knee. "Babe. Remember, we decided not to talk about that anymore. It isn't real."

"Oh yeah. That's right. Thanks for reminding me."

John smiled broadly.

"That was such a gracious exchange," he said. "I admire the two of you as a couple so much. Bill, I know that you will make a very good recovery."

Thursday, April 16

I stayed with John and Jeanne last night. Their place is closer to the highway, making my trip back a little shorter, and being in their company is wonderful.

You called about 6:00 yesterday evening, just before we sat down to one of Jeanne's delicious dinners. "I've had interesting meetings today. I walked with Phong this morning. I really enjoy that. Then I met with Doctor—you know who I mean—the doc whose name starts with G." (You have many names for Doctor Horn.) "He said that he thought I was making great progress, that I might be able to judge wines again. Then I met with John Gallagher and I talked to him about resuming marital relations. He thinks we are getting close to doing that. It's been a good day."

When I arrived this morning, you were sitting on the swing in the courtyard. You only acknowledged me when I stood in front of you, although you certainly saw me pull up and park.

"Hi Toots," you said. "I had a meeting with Brian this morning. I don't know if it's the Seroquel or what but I get so drowsy right after the meds. I almost fell asleep halfway through our session. He had me doing math and I just got lost. Lost! I had to ask him if he would help me rebuild what we were doing. He said he would. Sometimes I think I am about as far as I will go. And maybe that's okay. When I get back to Cape Coral and Watkins Glen, maybe just getting up in the morning and having breakfast on the patio, reading in the sun, talking, maybe that's all I need. You know, I've gotten happier here in the last couple of days. I've spoken to people in more depth and I asked Gallagher this . . ." You began to cry. We had to wait a minute for you to get control. "I asked him if all my knowledge of wine that I've built up over all these years is gone. I haven't dared ask that before. But he said, no, he didn't think so. He thinks it will come back." You smiled with tears running down your cheeks.

I put my arms around you and saw over your shoulder that you had been reading, *My Stroke of Insight*, the story of a woman who suffered a mammoth stroke, and her road back to recovery.

"I have sobbed through most of this," you said. "It is such a story of the human condition, of someone who once could do things, but now can't." A pause. "Let's get out of here."

You jumped up and headed to the apartment and returned with your swimsuit and a change of clothes in the hamper I'd just bought for dirty clothes. You got into the passenger's side of the car.

I slid in the driver's seat, just as you exclaimed, "Oh shit. I forgot my coffee."

You leapt out of the car and sprinted back to the apartment, emerging a moment later, mug in hand. As you pulled yourself back into the car, the top came off the mug, spilling hot coffee all over your pants.

"Oh come on, you stupid asshole. Stupid sonofabitch," you shouted at yourself.

When you returned wearing a clean pair of pants, I gently shook your shoulder and said, "I am going to get you in the sun. I think your mood will change."

You looked embarrassed. "I'm sure uptight."

As we changed into our swimsuits in my room at the hotel, you became sullen again. "Why can't I just stay here overnight? They've stripped me of everything. I feel like a goddamned child."

"Bill, when you got the whack on your head, you got sent back to childhood. 'They' haven't taken anything. The accident took it."

We moved outside to a table. "Do you know how much I hate this—including having my wife treat me like my mother?" you said with a sneer.

I moved to another table. You followed me to continue your harangue. "Well, how do you think it makes me feel? My wife sides with the doctors when it comes to our intimate life. You care more about them."

I tried to ignore you—keep writing in my journal. I am so tired of trying to explain all of this. And the damned guardianship will come up in a few days.

"Can you take me to the beach, please?"

"No, I can't take you to the beach now. We have just arrived here. You have a choice. We can enjoy a nice day or have a rotten one. We have the potential for a great one."

Your posture is that of a small boy. The incongruity is always jolting.

"Look, I don't want to continue beating up on you," you said. "But I can't even access my credit card for cash. I got shut out yesterday. Here. Please call the company and find out what's going on."

I called the credit card company. They said they must hear your voice. You apparently answered a question incorrectly so they asked for your driver's license. Oh, good, now you'll go on about not having your driver's license, which we are afraid to give you for fear you will run away and try to rent a car. You look downtrodden, sad, beaten. "I don't even have a cell phone."

Then I remember! "I have a surprise for you." I went to the car and returned with a TracFone. I called it from my phone to prove it was working. You were in seventh heaven.

"Thank you! Is this a birthday present?"

"No, it's just an 'I'm happy to be with you' gift. Last night I told John and Jeanne how frustrated you were that you didn't have a cell phone and John suggested this TracFone. It has a limited number of minutes so if you lose it, it won't be a big deal."

After lunch, you said, "I'm feeling kind of funny. Like I'm coming to the end of a period of time and now I need to do something else. We should revel in our successes, shouldn't we? I wasn't always a great spouse, or a good parent. I know that. I think I am experiencing an emotional side I never knew I had. It's so weird. I want to tell people I love them. You know? What a gift! I love you so much."

Sunday, April 19

My morning call at the hotel at 7:15. "Don't forget to bring my papers. I need them here on the base. Where are you?"

Kremers and Knotts are planning to visit today. These visits help me keep my sanity.

Going out for lunch always lifts your mood. Today is no exception. Peter referred to "going south" as something deteriorating. You leaned over with mock conspiracy and said, "Peter, it isn't politically correct to use that expression here in Florida."

Who'd have thought that a simple sentence like that could make us all look at one another in wonder. That was such a—well, intelligent, statement. First, it was funny. But even better, you know where we are.

When we arrived back on campus, you said, "Well, thanks for coming everybody. I think it's nap time for me." You went into your apartment, not inviting any of us to join you.

After our guests left, I walked in. You were sitting on the couch, reading. "I know what you're up to. You want to go back to the pool, don't you?"

A big smile. "I am so glad to be married to you. You understand me. You know my tolerance. I'm so lucky to have you. When you're not here, I feel like a kid abandoned at camp. I know that's childish, but that's how I feel."

Sitting by the pool, you began, "I want to talk to you about Gina and Renee. I can talk to them about everything, even things I wouldn't talk to you about."

Oh good Lord. "Like what?"

"Like anal penetration."

"What?!"

"That's just an outlandish example. I never really talked to them about it. But I could."

"Oh, Bill, Bill, Bill. Issues like that should be taken up with John Gallagher, who is trained to help you through some of those thoughts. Or even with Doctor Horn. Gina and Renee are not trained to talk to you about such things."

When we returned from the hotel, we sat out in the gazebo. I told you, "You know, the doctors are thinking that in a couple of weeks, you can come home to Cape Coral for a weekend. They want us to take a

157

staff person. If that works well, the following week, you will be discharged."

"Wow, what great news. I wonder how it will feel to return."

"Well, I am storing our wine and booze in a storage unit. You won't be able to drink for some time and I think it's good to remove all temptation."

"I wish you wouldn't do that. It will give the impression I am an alcoholic."

Hello . . .

Even though there are ups and down, your clarity seems to be returning.

"I've been reading in the papers that the economy has really tanked. Has that affected us?"

"Everyone's financial picture has darkened," I told you. "But we'll be all right."

Monday, April 20

We had a great staff meeting today. The doctors are very pleased with your progress and Doctor Horn reiterated that in about two weeks you can come to Cape Coral for the weekend. You are very excited. So am I. Is it possible that we can have a "normal" life again? I reflect on it being Mark's birthday and that I have not even sent a card.

During dinner at Sam Seltzer's tonight you drew a perfect floor plan of the Cape Coral house. Only two weeks ago, you asked me what in heaven I was doing in a place called Cape Coral. You had no memory of our house there.

You have realized how angry you are—and you have observed that many of the other patients are angry as well. You asked me to take you to Barnes and Noble where you picked out three books on anger management. This seems like a huge step but with this new clarity also comes more dangers. You proudly told me today you had called an 800 number and got the minutes on your TracFone increased.

Leaving you tonight was so difficult. You looked very handsome in your black open neck golf shirt and khaki pants. So "Bill." As you get more back to yourself, it seems almost outlandish that I have to say goodnight and return to the hotel I have come to hate. About 9:30 you called. "I took a test in the anger management book. It was about 80 questions. I'm not as bad as I thought! My problem is only moderate."

"Great. I told you at dinner tonight that when you make up your mind to do something, you do it."

"At dinner? We didn't have dinner together, did we?"

Two steps ahead. One back.

"Yes, remember, you had salmon and I had crab cakes."

"Oh, I thought that was lunch. I don't have a memory of you at dinner. Wait! I remember telling you about the guy in the rest room talking on his cell phone. But then it feels as if I walked alone through the parking lot . . ."

Is it the Seroquel, I wonder?

Wednesday, April 29

Andra, Marijn and the girls have come to visit you, so knowing you would have family with you I took the opportunity to return to Cape Coral. When I arrived back at Communicare this morning, it had been a week since we'd seen one another. You rushed out of the apartment and appeared very happy to see me. We walked out to the gazebo, where you became very emotional. "I want to thank you for all you have done. I know I wouldn't be here if it weren't for you. I want to do something special for you, but you know a string of pearls? I don't think that will express what I want to say."

I find myself not trusting these treks into lovingness, knowing how quickly the landscape changes.

Being away has given me a little fresher perspective. You are still childish—telling personal issues, some of which are not true, obsessing on your caretakers. You seem to have become "institutionalized," viewing Doctor Horn and others as your authority figures in an elementary school way. This indicates to me that it is time to spring you from this environment. Please God, give me the strength to deal with you alone.

You are still struggling with time and space, and this is very frustrating. "How do you just know it's Saturday?" you asked me. "I can't figure things like that out. I can't even subtract, do you know that?"

"We have been told that with the right therapy all of that will return, Bill. That is why it has been so important for you to stay here and keep working with your therapists. Many people go home before they are ready to cope. Then they become frustrated and depressed. Keep working, Babe. Keep working."

As heartbreaking as this is, it is also heartening. You have realized what you CAN'T do, and that is making you easier to work with in your sessions. Your speech therapist, Brian, has become someone you look forward to seeing and he is very pleased with the progress you have made.

Then your mood changes. "I don't trust Horn. I'm not sure he'll let me out. I think they see us as a cash cow. They want to keep me here. I don't dare think I am really going home in two weeks. I feel so forsaken. So lonely."

"I've been lonely, too, Bill."

"Yes, but you haven't had anything taken from you. You still have all your freedoms. I just want you to know how I feel. When are we planning to go back to Cape Coral?"

"Monday."

"Then, the following weekend I will come home?"

"Yes."

"You can't believe how relieved I am to have that Reiskind visit behind me. God, I was nervous. Thought he'd say I had to stay longer."

Doctor Reiskind is a physiologist, with whom you visited while you were still at Communicare. On your first visit you were charming. You regaled him with stories of how you were planning to give your speech to the Navy recruits' parents. You told him about your long career in the Navy and how proud you were of that. But, you said, you were sorry that you had re-upped without discussing it with the family.

The doctor, who it seemed had not read your records before our visit, turned to me and said, "This man seems to have made incredible strides toward recovery."

"Yes," I said. "If only anything that he just told you was true, we would be happy with his progress." The doctor stared at me for a minute, rifled through some papers on his desk, then turned to you. "Buddy, I would ditch that Navy stuff, if I were you. Here's how you do that. Whenever you have a thought about the Navy, you tell yourself to put it on the back burner."

That simple statement finally freed you from your Navy obsession.

The visit you had with him today went well. He was very pleased with the changes he'd seen in only two weeks. At the end of the visit, he said, "You talk a good case, Buddy. But keep working."

You were on a roll. The visits were all having positive implications.

"I also had a good visit with John Gallagher the other day," you told me. "I told him how much I appreciated all of the work my therapists have done with me. John said he really admired us as a couple. I told him how much fun we have had when we got away from the facility and he was pleased."

"I talk to Renee a lot, too," you continued. "She is quite a gal. I think she can do a lot to improve Communicare. She has a lot on the ball, and you know she cares deeply about me. I think we might have a business project we can do together."

"Bill, I think you are obsessing over Renee."

You gaze, grimace, then nod in seeming agreement.

I said, "Remember in the meeting with John Gallagher, I said that I thought you'd been almost physically held up with so much love? You leapt to the conclusion that I was talking about your caretakers. I was talking about our family, our friends, and me. It hurt my feelings that you only thought about Renee and Gina."

"Oh, I'm sorry. I missed that one. I feel bad when I miss things like that. But I don't remember any of the kids visiting. Only Andra."

You have no memory of the long months we all stood by your bedside at Lee Memorial and at HealthSouth. Your first reality dawned here at Communicare.

Friday, May 1

We had a long meeting with Doctor Horn yesterday. He explained the reason for the guardianship to you, and took most of the credit for insisting it be put in place. He said he wrote the letter for me to take to the lawyer himself. He stressed this would be a temporary measure, but one important for the protection of our finances until your mind is clear enough to make appropriate decisions. You were impassive.

Then Doctor Horn said he saw no reason you couldn't come and spend the weekend at the hotel with me. We are both elated.

Tonight, after dinner at the little Chinese restaurant across the highway in the mall, we fell in bed about 9:00 p.m., both of us bushed. We slept ten hours! That is the longest you have slept since you came here. We woke up, gently holding one another, feeling in wonder. We are getting our life back.

I drove us to Indian Beach where we walked for over an hour, then went to the Columbia Restaurant for lunch. You are always happy there.

I need to return to Cape Coral for a few days to catch up on paperwork. Maybe I'll sleep round the clock one of those days.

Friday, May 8

The court-appointed attorney visited you today at Communicare, concerning the guardianship, and although Doctor Horn sat in, and tried to help you understand, you dug in your heels. You would sign nothing. You called me after the meeting. "When it was painted in pastels," you said, "it didn't seem so foreboding. But looking at the goddamned documents, you know the lawyers are in it again. I don't want any more lawyers pulling us apart. And this will become an issue for us. If you want me to sign something that says I can't make purchases, I think you should give up your rights, too. Both of us should have to sign for the other. What if you decided to run off with the lawyer? You could take all the money . . ."

I was stunned. I know. I know. Brain injury. But it stings.

Sunday, May 10, Mother's Day

You are on your way here to Cape Coral at this moment, driven by Renee. I am excited, scared, feel like crying. I wonder how you will react. If this goes well, you will come home next weekend for good.

We have been working hard to make your homecoming both pleasant and safe. I had a railing installed on the stairs down to the canal from the lanai, and Chris painted the steps and the dock. I had grab bars installed in the shower, and tried to remove anything that seemed like it posed a risk, like throw rugs.

Within minutes of your arrival, Renee said she had friends in the area she wanted to look up. She said she'd be back in a couple of hours. I was grateful for her understanding and tact. You and I went out to the lanai. Sitting there by the pool, looking out over the canal, you seemed in seventh heaven. You just grinned. "Hoo boy. I am happy to be home."

I pray you won't push too hard for your credit cards, for your password to get into all of our financial accounts, to drive, or for access to alcohol. I have no backups now. I am excited over this next step, having you here at home, but I am scared, too. This will be a challenge, and I pray I'm up to it.

I have been forced to take over everything you once did, and you say this makes you feel emasculated. But the experience has made me much more independent. I'm sure this will create issues for us. I am nervous, trying not to show it.

The rest of the weekend went without a hitch. When you walked down the steps to the canal, I could not resist peeking to be sure you were okay. But mostly we hung out by the pool. "Our own pool," you said quite a few times, sighing and smiling.

Monday, May 11

Renee was off by 7:00 this morning, but you and I were a little more leisurely, leaving about 9:00. You would not return to your apartment at Communicare, but would stay at the hotel with me.

Sunday had gone so well that I called Doctor Horn and told him I didn't see why you couldn't return home to Cape Coral with me after the meeting with him and the new attorney on Tuesday instead of waiting until next weekend. He agreed.

Still, the guardianship issue is hanging over our heads. You had taken an immediate dislike to the first attorney sent to represent you, and you had refused to deal with her. Doctor Horn has arranged for another attorney to join us in tomorrow's meeting so we could have this issue resolved before returning to Cape Coral.

Tuesday, May 12

Before your new lawyer arrived at Doctor Horn's office for the meeting, you began, "I have given a great deal of thought to this guardianship thing, and I am not happy about it at all. I don't think I am going to sign papers that take away all of my rights."

Doctor Horn remained laid back, but authoritative. "Bill, this is just a temporary measure. You are still unpredictable, and you could do great harm to the stability of your entire family, and then deeply regret it later. It is for your protection as well."

You remained unconvinced, staring with a dark scowl out the window.

The receptionist, Brie, came in to tell us that the lawyer was waiting in the reception area.

Doctor Horn nodded, and continued talking quietly.

You erupted. "No, goddammit, I am tired of being pushed on this. I think if SHE," you nodded in my direction, "wants to take away all of my rights, SHE should have hers taken away, too."

Brie re-entered. "The lawyer said she wouldn't wait any longer. She left."

(She would, of course, bill us for her time.)

I was out of steam. I didn't know what to do next. This godforsaken guardianship was costing thousands of dollars and now we were back to square one. No—farther back. We didn't have the guardianship in place, and you thought I was the enemy.

I said to Doctor Horn, "I want to get out of here and take Bill home. I just want to get out."

"How about staying one more day?" Doctor Horn asked.

"No. I have had it. I want to go home."

By the time we reached your apartment I was sweating more heavily than I have ever done before. Sweat was dripping off my face, off my arms. I felt weak, and hungry.

"Let's go to the cafeteria and get something to eat before we take off."

You looked amazed and disdainful. "You really think that on my last day here I want to sit in the cafeteria and have lunch? I'm going to go out on my regular walk. I want to do it one more time."

You have made my life miserable with your hatred of this place, your constant begging to come home, and now that we are finally about to

167

leave, you are feeling nostalgic?

I wanted to strangle you. I grabbed a slice of bread from the refrigerator, slathered it with peanut butter and gulped it down with a little tea. Then I felt nauseated.

Rotanda came over to ask if we could wait a few more minutes so we could sign paperwork. Also, she thought some of the therapists would like to see you this afternoon.

I would not wait until late afternoon, and then face commuter traffic all the way back to Cape Coral. I was hitting the wall.

I began to lug things from your apartment to the Explorer. I knew I was acting manic.

You finished your walk and came to help me load. "Maybe we should stay at the hotel tonight," you said calmly. "We can drive home tomorrow."

"I am not staying one more night in that fucking hotel. We are going home! Get in."

I didn't reflect until later on the fact that now I was sounding crazy and you sane!

Without thinking of saying goodbye and thanking all of the people who have helped us here, I hit the gas and we were on our way. I knew it was dangerous for me to be driving, feeling as shaky as I did, but I couldn't help myself. I wanted to go home! And I never wanted to see that place again.

I think what I really wanted was for everything to turn normal. I didn't know if I could take anymore.

I had set the GPS, but the voice instructions made you nervous. "Do you really have to listen to this after all the times you have driven this route?"

I was embarrassed to admit that, yes, I still depended on this device we have dubbed "Maggie," (for Magellan). But I shut her off. Anything for peace.

Close to Sarasota, the skies opened up—the way they often do in Florida in the afternoon in summer. Cars were pulling off the road under every bridge. I thought that was dangerous. It felt safer keeping going.

"I'd like to suggest that you drive a little less aggressively," you said calmly. "Your windshield wipers aren't able to keep up with the rain, and if you go slower you will be able to see better."

Why is it, I wonder, that when I am about out of control, you suddenly turn calm and with-it?

Between Sarasota and Cape Coral the rain ceased. I felt calmer. We stopped at the Publix in Cape Coral to pick up something for dinner.

Am I ready to start this new phase of our life?

Better be, I think. Not much choice.

Wednesday, June 3

Being at home with you the last couple of weeks has not been a picnic. We make plans to go someplace, and then you either forget or change your mind about wanting to go, often just as we are going out the door.

You say you feel "demotivated." That is your new word.

There are breakthroughs, though—causes for celebration.

We went to Lowe's and bought a chest for storing cushions and pool toys which we plan to keep out on the lanai. It came disassembled, and when you pulled out the parts, I went into the house to stay out of your way. After about an hour and a half, you proclaimed your job done. You had followed all of the instructions, and put the thing together! We called your speech therapist, Brian, who was delighted. "That's just the kind of thing I want him to keep doing," he said. "Keep the jobs challenging!"

Although you have made great strides over the couple of weeks you have been home, we have decided to sell this house, as much as we love it. We agreed that maintaining it and our house in New York is more than we can comfortably handle right now. Having it listed means we have to keep it spick and span and need to leave when the agents want to show it. Never knowing what mood you will be in makes this a challenge.

Your moodiness is one of our biggest issues. I never know what to expect. You are often cutting and sarcastic in your remarks.

It's so hard to know where the brain injury stops and "Bill" begins. For a reason I can't fathom, you have decided that you hate my brothers. You don't want to see John and Fran and although you say you don't blame John for the accident, you are angry with him. You were barely civil to Art and Di when they were here for an overnight. I told you how much they had done for you, for us. You responded, "I didn't ask for it."

But when the six of us went to breakfast, you made a little speech, thanking them for taking care of me, and of you. With tears in his eyes, Art said, "Di and I made some sacrifices, but we couldn't fathom how Hope was able to deal with everything for so many months. Your wife is the one you should be thanking." You acted as if you hadn't heard.

A new lawyer was assigned to your case to deal with the guardianship. She came to visit, and this one you liked. She set a court date for the following week.

John and Fran drove us to the Courthouse in Fort Myers. We were greeted there by lawyer, Lance McKinney, the lawyer Chas and I had met with last month. You warmly shook his hand.

We were seated in the front row of the empty courtroom, and the judge asked you if you understood what these proceedings were about.

You nodded that you did.

"You are willingly giving the power to handle your finances to your wife?"

I thought, come on; let's not drag this out!

But you chuckled a little and said, "You know, she always was better with money that I was."

You never know—but another thanks, Lord.

We learned later this guardianship issue is fraught with danger in unexpected ways. Many financial institutions refuse to continue to do business with a family that has a guardianship in place. They fear, apparently, that they are open to suit if one of their representatives doesn't check the records thoroughly enough, and allows a person under a guardianship to make a withdrawal or do any other business. Charles Schwab and our financial advisors, Burns & Matteson, thank goodness, hung in there with us.

Your speech therapist, Brian, had suggested a therapy he has found very successful in helping brain-injured patients make a recovery. It is called interactive metronome, and only a few people are licensed to administer it. I found one in Bonita Springs, about a 45-minute drive from Cape Coral. We have been making that drive three times a week for several weeks. I swear you have been better at knowing the day of the week already.

Here's how it works: The therapist has a computer set up on a table. Attached to it are two sets of earphones, one for her and one for you. The computer screen is divided into three sections. You both hear metronomic sounds through the earphones, and she asks you to clap your hands in time with the beat. Your claps are recorded on the screen, in the left third if you are clapping more slowly than the metronome beat, middle if you are right on, and in the right third if you are fast.

Time is measured in milliseconds, so this is very challenging and requires focus. In the second session, she introduced another motion, hitting your own thigh in time with the metronome. She explained that she would continue adding new motions, later including your legs and feet.

One day, you told me you know that you are not contributing to any of the household tasks, but when I ask you to do so, you ignore me.

I think I may have to push this more because I do not want to spend the rest of my life waiting on you and cleaning up after you. I know you are capable of more than you are doing, but I think you find it comfortable to just do what you want to do—and let me clean up the mess.

Monday, June 14

The phone rang at 5:00 a.m. with news of the birth of our new grand-daughter, Lucca Serena. We heard her first sounds! I ache to be here. Heaven knows how long it will be before I can make the trek across the country to California to meet her. But what a thrill to be THERE as she was brand new to the world.

Today we went to buy a file cabinet at Office Max. As soon as we were out the door of the store, you turned to me and said, "I don't know if you noticed or not, but I remembered our New York address and phone number, and our Florida address and phone number. It was hard not to tell that clerk what I just accomplished!"

I had kept our friends and relatives updated on your recovery for many months during your recuperation using the wonderful website, CaringBridge. I had two sites, one for family and another for friends and colleagues. The family site was more specific. That afternoon, you asked me to bring up the CaringBridge site on the computer, and our friends heard directly from you for the first time.

Dear friends,

I want to thank you very much for checking in with the CaringBridge website or visiting me or otherwise staying in touch by letter, internet mail, card or telephone. Your personal contact has meant a great deal to me and Hope who in some cases learned of it well before I was able to receive or process your message. It became a real day brightener for me as I learned of it and it helped me pull out of the emotional hole I was in following the accident we had while vacationing in Florida in late December.

Hope's brother and his wife were in the front seats when the accident occurred. Fortunately, none of us was so seriously injured that we envision long-lasting impairment from the accident. The good news is that Hope, while banged hard by the car that collided with ours, has made a full recovery already. The accident broke some of my ribs and neck and made me a traumatic brain injury case, which admittedly sounds kind of scary but as a Blake and U of M (University of Minnesota) student I've received worse report cards. I was in and out of the hospital for nursing and cognitive rehab for close to five months up in Clearwater, FL at a place whose staff specializes in head injury rehabilitation. Hope spent many nights in Clearwater and in Sarasota visiting with me (without many kudos from her husband, the impatient patient). Now we've been released from there and we're ensconced in our winter home in Cape Coral, FL and life begins—just begins—to seem a little normal for the first time in five

173

months. The general consensus is that I am coming along nicely, as Hope has reported well to you on CaringBridge. I'm waiting for more rehab and cognitive redevelopment, which will largely take place at our home in upstate New York. Hope and I are flying that way soon. One of the outstanding tools in my reconstruction has been a newish device called the Interactive Metronome, and I expect to pick that up again when we get to New York. If you want more info on that device, you can Google it! And before I forget my manners, I want to say that I am deeply indebted to our family who came (some with their kids!) from as far away as California to visit and who stood by me during much of my recuperation; also to the staff of caregivers at the Clearwater and Sarasota care units.

Since my team of doctors, led by Gordon Horn, has put alcohol of any source—even wine!—off my list for at least another month while my brain heals from the impact I made with the car's dashboard, it is really too soon to talk very particularly about my professional future. Both of us hate to lose seeing and having rapport with the many friends we have made in the industry and getting back to that is as much of an imperative as it can be. The good news is that at this point, none of the attending docs are ruling out a full recovery for me, or a return to wine as an interest if not profession. But it looks like Bill's glass will have to stay mostly unfilled for a while longer (meals and cooking have been a drag so far)! Though she has joined me in temperance, Hope's tasting has not been affected and she is raring and able to go as soon as the right professional venue appears! On the imperative side, whether in wine, sailing or business or in just sitting around the campfire (which sounds pretty nice imagining you there), we want to see you ASAP. We will try to keep you posted as things mature for us.

As winter gives over to whatever is the next season where you live, the rainy season has begun here in SW Florida. It looks like we will be in Florida through mid-June and then return to Seneca Lake in NY for what will be left of the sailing season. Our good friends, John Kremer and Peter Knott have already put our sailboat in the water, a Catalina 30 called Calaloo, named after a spicy Caribbean chicken, corn and vegetable stew. We expect to clamber aboard before too much more of the sailing season goes by.

Taking a longer view of things, we hope to rejoin the wine world in 2010. But we will plan on seeing you around the campfires long before then!

Thanks again for communicating your caring to us. Hope joins me in sending you love in return from Cape Coral, Florida.

Bill Moffett

Our friends were overjoyed to hear from Bill directly, many sending uplifting messages: "Hip hip hooray! Welcome back, Bill!" and "OMG, thank you so much! You're back."

Hope's Epilogue
Canandaigua, 2016

I had intended to end this book here until as the months, then years, passed I realized this is an ongoing story. There will probably not be a simple happy ending.—I have learned that in life there seldom is.

Though our home in Florida had not yet sold, we returned to Watkins Glen in late June 2009.

Several of our children and grandchildren met us at the airport with a grand welcome, holding up handmade signs proclaiming, "Welcome Home Papa Bill and Grandma Hope!"

When we arrived home, they insisted we rest while they barbecued steaks, and served them with all the trimmings—baked potatoes, salad, and green beans. It was so like old times. It felt as if we'd been gone for years.

After the kids left, we went out onto our deck overlooking lovely Seneca Lake. We sat holding hands, sighing and smiling.

For a few minutes it felt that life might be normal again.

I have been reminded frequently of the day during his rehab that Bill said, "You keep saying everything will be all right, but I don't think so. I think the Bill you once knew won't be back. Someone with a brain injury like mine will probably never be the same. You may be waiting for a bus that never comes into the station." I wonder how he had such insight given the severity of his brain injury.

The Bill I once knew never did come back. I am still getting used to the "new" Bill.

The old Bill wasn't happy unless he had numerous projects going at once: building something in his woodworking shop, tending his garden, rebuilding part of the house, planning a vacation.

The new Bill sleeps late, and has difficulty becoming motivated. Once he begins a new project, and has done it for a while, it sometimes becomes habitual enough he can sustain his interest and action. But interrupt that—with a trip, for instance—and picking it back up is very difficult for him.

Here's an example: He had been attending cardio rehab three times a week for several months. He was getting stronger and gaining better balance, and he enjoyed it. His progress was measured, and this has always been important to him. In February, 2010, after several months of his investment in rehab, we traveled to California to be near our son and granddaughters for two and a half weeks. Well into March, I still hadn't been able to get him back to the gym.

I have to remember that Bill has been through several serious hospitalizations in the six years since the accident, including open heart surgery in October of 2009, just eight months after the accident, and colon cancer surgery in 2012. All of this has weakened him, as it would any seventy plus year old. It is hard to know what is caused by the brain injury, what is fatigue, and what is his old stubbornness coming back into play.

During the months following the accident and his surgeries, he'd been adhering to an alcohol-free life—but not happily. On one visit to our doctor, he was bitterly complaining about the loss he felt. The doctor said he thought it would be all right if he had a glass of wine with dinner. "Just try it," he said. "See if you can enjoy that glass of wine, but keep it to that."

This quickly became a slippery slope. Soon Bill was having several glasses of wine, and then he added the martini before dinner he used to always enjoy. Soon he was having a "nightcap," and then he had a "splash" of vodka in the morning, and it went even farther downhill from there.

In May of 2014 he awoke one morning with a terrible stomachache that had kept him up during the night. I found him sitting on the couch in misery. Our primary care doctor admitted him to the hospital and he was quickly diagnosed with acute pancreatitis. He was in the hospital for a week, off food and liquids, fed intravenously.

The doctors were unequivocal in their prognosis. "If you continue to drink alcohol, you will die."

Though I knew this was medically necessary for him, it was a bitter pill for both of us to swallow. Much of our lives had revolved around wine.

Beginning in 1975, and for the next 30 years, we had published a trade magazine that focused on growing grapes and producing wine. Our company sponsored several wine judgings and we judged wines in other events all over the country. Our company also sponsored, and we led, wine tours to France and Germany and all over the U.S. Wine defined us in many ways. Our son now owns the company and operates it out of his California office.

I cannot believe that we can no longer participate in the wine judging

176

events sponsored by our company, or attend as judges at other events. We live here in wine country, surrounded by wineries we'd love to visit, but now we don't dare. So, a huge part of our life has been cut out. Nevertheless, he has been alcohol free for ten months,—not a small feat for a TBI survivor, and one whose lifetime career revolved around wine.

We have lived through an emotional and physical typhoon. You might think that would have made us closer, but—I am struggling here to explain—it has instead, forged a distance between us. This, too, I have learned, is not unusual after one partner suffers traumatic brain injury.

The children find him sweeter and kinder and his social skills have remained intact, allowing us to continue to have friendships among old and new circles of friends. Among a group of friends he is often the bon vivant. Though he often eschews get-togethers, once there, he seems stimulated by the comradery.

I reflect on what a neurologist said years ago: "If you and he go to a party nobody there will know about his brain injury. It won't be obvious. Only you will know it because you will live with it every day."

For many years we've loved to sail. We made many friends through sailing. But the summer we returned home, walking down the dock to our boat and then boarding it required a lot of effort for him, and sailing was out of the question. "I refuse to be a 'dock sailor'," he proclaimed, referring to some folks who use their boat as a cottage to the derision of the "hard core" sailors. Our 30-foot Catalina, Calaloo, sat sadly unused the entire season. The next season promised to be more of the same, so we placed her on the market. Luckily, we found a buyer quickly, a young fellow, with a wife and small daughter, so thrilled with his new purchase it buoyed our spirits to think of Calaloo once again romping on the waves of Lake Ontario.

But Bill seemed lost. All of the activities in life that had once given him pleasure had been taken away. He was no longer publisher of a wine and grape trade publication, a career he'd enjoyed so much. He couldn't judge wines anymore, which he'd loved doing. He couldn't work in his woodworking shop where he'd built a beautiful swinging cradle for our grandson and many other remarkable creations. He couldn't garden.

"Who am I?" he asked our counselor.

"You are Bill Moffett," our counselor responded. "The essence of you is still the same."

He couldn't make sense of that. He was no longer Publisher Bill, Gardener Bill, Wine Judge Bill, Woodworker Bill. Without these activities he

177

seemed to have no identity to which to cling.

In 2012 I decided it was time for us to downsize our living situation. Without Bill's contribution to the maintenance of our home and grounds, I had hired more and more help. It was getting expensive. Also we had a steep driveway treacherous in winter if we didn't go out every few hours to keep it salted during snowstorms. It had become more than we could handle.

I investigated many kinds of senior living situations and discovered an apartment facility in Canandaigua, Ferris Hills, which seemed perfect for us.

One of the last nights we were in Watkins Glen, I woke up and realized that Bill was not in the bed. He was sitting on the couch in the living room. When he saw me coming down the hall, he motioned to me to come and sit next to him.

"Do you recognize me?" he asked.

I tried not to show my shock or sadness. "Of course, I recognize you. You are my husband."

"Good. I recognize you, too. Could you please tell me what we are doing here?"

I felt profound sadness.

"This is our home," I said.

"You know, I thought so. But I can't quite feel it."

I remembered the diagram he'd made for his speech therapist, Brian, back at his rehab facility, Communicare, when he'd drawn a small circle with "Bill" written inside, and another larger circle, where he'd written "the world." He had told Brian he knew the world was there, but he couldn't quite get in it.

We sat quietly for a few minutes, holding hands, before he said, "You explain things well to me. Thank you for that."

We rented an apartment at Ferris Hills for three months on a trial basis. That led to our decision to buy the apartment, and make Ferris Hills our permanent home.

We were in the process of moving there in April of 2013. This necessitated making the trek back to Watkins Glen often, to oversee the packing, and deciding what to take with us, what went to the kids, and which of our things went to the Salvation Army.

It was a huge job, made worse by my having to pull Bill out of bed on the days we needed to go from one place to the other. He would often

drag his heels and when I begged him to hurry, he'd respond, "I'm retired. I don't have to hurry!" He was drinking so heavily by then that he
didn't grasp most of what was happening around him.

On Easter weekend I decided we would spend the entire weekend in
Watkins Glen. It would give me several days to work, but I also wanted
to participate in the Easter rites at St. Mary's of the Lake Church.

At about 3:00 a.m. Sunday, I was awakened by strange violent moving
of the bed and realized that he was having a seizure. This was his third,
so I now knew what was happening. I called 911. I requested the ambulance take him to the Arnot Ogden Hospital in Elmira, about 30 miles
away, instead of the local Schuyler Hospital. My plan was that we would
be near our primary care provider, Doctor Dayakar Reddy.

Once he was settled in, I went to the lobby where I could get cell-
phone power, and tried to call Doctor Reddy. It wasn't until I had
reached his voicemail several times that I remembered this was Easter
Sunday. Then to make matters worse, Doctor Reddy had taken his family
on a weeklong trip since this was also spring vacation for his children.

Bill was kept at Arnot Hospital for about a week. Then I was able to
get him admitted to the Ewing Center, part of Thompson Hospital near
our new home in Canandaigua. Here he would receive Physical Therapy
to help him regain the strength he had lost during his hospital stay.

Once again Chas came to be with me to help me with the gigantic job
of moving us from a home we'd lived in for 23 years to a much smaller
apartment. He suggested we try to move the date of our transition to
Canandaigua up so that by the time Bill was dismissed from the Ewing
Center, I could take him directly to our new home. Chas felt, correctly
so, that Bill would have enough adjusting without having to move twice.

It was a scramble, but on the following rainy Monday, our house was
teeming with people packing boxes, others slogging through mud to
carry them out to the moving van. That night Chas and I slept in the new
apartment, before he had to leave the next day to return to his Long
Island home and to his teaching schedule at Hunter College. Two days
later I brought Bill home.

He was delighted to see all of our old furniture and artwork, and loved
the paint, carpeting and countertops I'd chosen. However, he told me a
few days later that he felt as if he had fallen asleep and when he awakened, he lived in Canandaigua. In the first months, he asked me often,
"When are we going home?"

Gradually, he came to grips with his new surroundings. I'd furnished the guest room with a desk for his computer, and a reclining chair with a good reading lamp by the window where he could look out over the woods and meadows. At the other end of the apartment, I have my own little office.

We found the people here wonderfully welcoming, and also sensitive to privacy needs. At first, we enjoyed cocktail hours, a tradition here, but after Bill had to give up alcohol, we needed to back off that activity. Maybe later he will be comfortable around others who are drinking.

We both enjoy our proximity to Rochester, New York, the home of the Eastman and Hochstein schools of music. This gives us access to world class concerts. We attend many plays, at the downtown Geva Theater. Our new home, Ferris Hills, is on over 50 acres with a walking trail through woods where it is not uncommon to see several deer, many varieties of songbirds, and interesting flower and berry bushes.

Last month we went back to Watkins Glen to have lunch with friends, and returning to Canandaigua that day Bill remarked, "This is the first time I have left Watkins Glen, feeling as if we are heading home, not leaving home."

My brother wrote, asking how I was doing. This was my response:

Dear Chas,

My last letter was pretty flip. Sometimes I feel like that. Everything is on an even keel.

Watching Celtic Women on WSKG tonight, I was so choked up that I knew that a lot of emotions are being buried, but are very near the surface.

Mostly, I feel we are so incredibly lucky I can't believe it.

But sometimes, when Bill looks very vulnerable and says something like, "Would you help me here with this? I can't seem to make my way through it."—about something that before the accident was a slam dunk for him—the sadness just sweeps over me.

Fact is we are still making headway. I notice that even his short term memory is getting better and better. I should dance in the streets.

The church has become such an anchor for me. Most of that is due to the wonderful priest in Watkins Glen, Father Paul Bonacci, who welcomed me so warmly back to the church. Very different from when I was Catholic before.

If I thought of Bill and me alone in the world, this accident would have continued to loom as a huge catastrophe.

But when I expand that vision a little, and remember the days after the accident, I have to define it in another way. Family came together. Our children learned that they loved Bill in a way they could not express before. My children and stepchildren were incredibly loving and supportive.

When I think about how you and Art and Di and John and Fran all came together, however they could, and supported me in so many ways, held me up really— then how can one not define this differently? How can I not say that so much love and good surfaced, perhaps, because of this accident?

But when I expand it even farther and remember that I am a child of the universe—or remember that I am a child of God—then, I feel small, but not diminished.

Small in the sense of belonging to a huge circle of human beings. Each of us has our burdens to bear, and our glories. When I think about what everyone else in the world is dealing with, I have to simply ask again, how can I handle the life I have been handed with grace, with courage, and with gratitude?

I think someday soon, I may have the damnedest cry the world has ever seen. Then, I think I will go on with life, grateful for all that I have and have been given.

Love,
Hope

Bill's Epilogue[1]

A remarkable thing about being brain injured is that you don't know how badly you're hurt—except in retrospect, which is to say after you have been told about it. Also true, having your memory out to lunch makes it challenging to find a place to start any account of being dumbed-down in a car wreck. Long term, my intent here is to relate as much as I can of the injured person's experience. Together my wife, Hope, and I want to give you this "inside" perspective in the case that you need a viewpoint to augment your own experience at some unfortunate time in the future. Bill, the injured husband, now talking. What I know now:

It was December of 1997[2]. My wife and I had just retired from our own business and had bought a retirement home in Florida. The night of the incident we were on our way out to dinner with family members when another vehicle plowed into ours. To me it wasn't dramatic or momentous, it just happened. I have no memory of it. My awareness—at least I believe to this day that this memory was prior to the reconstruction of my mind that followed—is that I had just unclasped my seatbelt buckle to sit forward from the backseat to give by wife's brother, the driver, directions to the restaurant to which we were headed. We were traversing an intersection that was locally-known as a dangerous corner.

---

[1] *Please Note:*

It seemed important to leave Bill's recount just as he remembered it, but to clear up confusion I'd like to point out areas where his memory does not fit with the facts.

I add these notes not only to clarify for the reader who has read a different version of these events in the body of the book, but also to allow readers to understand the confusion of memories that remain in the mind of a brain-injured person.

Which is not to say that I feel superior. Memory is a complicated thing with many layers. Even those of us that have not sustained a traumatic brain injury can remember the same event in different ways. This is why eyewitness testimony cannot always be relied on. In addition I had the advantage of writing down the events daily in a journal.

It is perhaps unusual for a brain-injured patient to have been a writer and to maintain those talents, therefore to be able to draw the kaleidoscopic picture he has drawn.

I have added footnotes with the clarifications below.

Hope

[2] *Bill lists the date of our accident as 1997. It was 2008. One result of his brain injury that stays with him today is his inability to remember dates clearly, or often to know what the date is. We have several tools to deal with that including an alarm clock on his night stand that displays the date, day and year.*

My first post-crash awareness is lying in the grass in the median[3], as if I were out of body and seeing myself from above. I don't know how that could have been possible! But that's where my story starts. What I will relate of the next few days is what I have pieced together from what others have told me about what was going on before my memory began kicking in and of intimate interaction with elements of my new environment. And also what I actually do remember. You'll have to give me some room here for post-crash amnesia.

For example, I remember an early memory being on site at the hospital[4] (what turned out to be my residence for several months—it felt sort of homey—I remember at the time) my wife telling me, no, she was not staying with me, because it was not allowed. I needed to get better!

I didn't understand.

I was disappointed and scared—my wife was where home is!

Am I staying in this strange place alone!?

This new unfamiliar place was to become my home until I was better, whatever that meant! The place was neat, it had two bedrooms, a kitchen and bath and it looked like a motel for the two of us. But it would not be such until I was better, whatever that meant! That's when it began to dawn on me that I was hurt worse than I felt.

Memories like this one make this part of our story a little awkward to relate. Much of my mind today remembers, if that is the right word to use, that things otherwise were about normal, however surreal, with strange comings and goings of people I did not know or expect, and doing so at odd hours. I remember that I sometimes became distressed and angry at these interruptions.

Oh, well . . .

Thank heaven for the caring and able staff of Communicare who were able to understand much of my handicap and explain, without really doing so, that I was a bit of a basket case needing TLC. They often used finesse to get me through the rough spots of being the emotional equivalent of a hole in the wall.

Only after a couple of meetings with the whole staff did it begin to dawn that this was all about me. My JOB was to get better!

---

[3] *Though Bill has pictured us on the median after we were hit, we were actually thrown across the road into a ditch.*

[4] *Bill's "entrance into the hospital" is his admittance to Communicare about two months after the accident.*

Nevertheless, my ambition here is to tell you, from this faulted perspective, that a comeback is possible (though you may not remember it later!).

I have learned that all I needed was a devoted wife, loving children and extended family members and exceptionally caring friends from all over the place who laid on hands and give words of encouragement throughout to help nurture. Otherwise I was fine! Unknowingly my mental and physical rehab from that of roadside vegetable to some semblance of my former self as writer, publisher and entrepreneur gradually started to return.

I say "all" above with tongue in cheek, of course. A large part of me feels I deserve to be still lying in that grass in the median from where the helicopter team of medics began my return to "reality "as we know it.

Even at this point some seven years later, my slate of memory is marked only by dull strokes. I have to rely on memories of all those above and others to start making some sense of who, or perhaps, "what" I was. I have now seen pictures of myself in those days. I am hooked to so many life support systems that I look more like a questionable lab experiment. It tells me today that both there was someone there who loved me and also someone who knew how to figure out all the wires and tubes!

It may be of interest to you, as we look for a starting place, that the first book I read after finding myself inexplicably in a rehab facility, was *In an Instant*, by Lee and Bob Woodruff. Their book retells the story of television reporter, Bob, whose brain injury comeback from a terrorist-placed roadside bomb during his reporting work in Iraq in the Gulf Conflict, made return to work iffy. Of a tragic and terrific wartime experience, the book was easy reading with a sense of personal identification, I remember having a sense of accomplishment, being myself a reader and a sometimes author. In essence, the book relates a horrifying personal experience and often details how Bob's wife, Lee, helped him get through.

Bottom line, Bob Woodruff was blown up in the truck when their vehicle ran over an IED bomb. He ended with severe brain injury which caused him to need to relearn all his skills to get on the come-back road as a TV journalist. His savior was truly his wife, Lee, as mine, Hope, was to me. Hope nursed me and guided family members to give me strength to hit the road on my feet again.

Though I have read Hope's manuscript twice, the presence and contributions of family and friends are, to this day, only shadows in my mind. have learned of some of them as time has gone by. You will learn of ome of them herein. Don't assume by my omissions that I am by nature ingracious or not thankful. They just didn't make it back to the book eeper's inbox.

By the way, I am more or less wholly sane today, but I have said to riends on numerous occasions, that if it hadn't been for my wife, Hope, might still be lying in the grass of that median today. I say this here to emind you of that first step after waking from a dream—that first step s both iffy and hard to separate from the dream. It gets better with time, oth wherever you are now or in the grass.

My memory bank holds random-seeming occasions of places and vents, beginning with that occasion lying in the median. Speaking of vhich, I believe I was told by a paramedic onsite that a chopper was oming in for me. I think I heard the whop-whop-whop of the prop.

I recall them being vague about where my wife was. They wouldn't ell me much about her.[5] All they would say was "Oh, she's being taken are of by another team."

I vaguely recall being lifted onto a gurney and placed in the plane. Hope was not there. I have no memory of the flight, darn it! Said like hat, because I was and still am an airplane buff.

However, I recall that I was told later that the plane didn't get to the ospital first. And when I asked again I was told that Hope was taken to nother place by ambulance. I had no idea then where I was but was told ater that it was Memorial Hospital in Fort Myers, Florida.

Several days of being zoned out followed, of hospital images fuzzy nd indistinct as to treatment and circumstances. Next I was transferred y ambulance up to Clearwater, I think, and there I received a double raniotomy to relieve pressure on my brain.

Then I think I was transferred again to a facility called Communicare n Clearwater whose specialty was caring for and rehabbing brain injuries.

Here we talked in hushed voices that "this is where they bring injured ro footballers" for repair! This became my therapeutic home for several

---

Bill was in a coma after the accident and thus could not have actually asked about me. I believe hat after reading the manuscript in which I repeatedly asked for him, he transposed the event to emember himself asking for me. It is possible that he had an "out of body" experience, and saw himself rom above, but it is more likely that after reading about the accident, in his mind's eye, he became the erson on the ground.

months and where I gradually began to recover snips of memory.

It is nearly impossible to form a continuum but I have salient memories—some I am proud of, some I am not—not the least of which was growing to believe my wife was leaving me to my own devices, which she certainly was not. Nor is it noble of me to have become so enamored of two care givers that they came to seem at times more caring than my wife.

That can be symbolic of brain injury induced "thinking" and along with that a most worrisome feeling of emasculation coming from absences of typical privileges for one's age because of care givers' caution about your normalcy of abilities. All reasonable and normal—but not.

I questioned why I was being treated for weeks before it began to dawn on me that I was not the same guy as the one going out to dinner a couple weeks ago!

In truth, my life was changing long before I really knew it.

I just really didn't care that much. I just went along with it.

That is, up until I sat in on a meeting between my wife, the doc and an attorney about signing papers to switch my customary head of household status to Hope in case I became unable or untrustworthy to act on our behalf. THAT was a wakeup call!

Later that day I talked by phone with our financial adviser several states away and that confirmed to me that I was in trouble and that we needed the additional security to be safe.

But it took me a long while to get over what seemed like the effrontery of being replaced.

A typical day at the facility from which I received most reconstructive instruction was fairly benign, though I had a desire to overlay a military institution character. If anything it was anything but—more hospital in general operation but nevertheless institutional—and all the rules were new to me!

My day was not rigidly structured but I was reminded of a sort of ranking system of which I was a part. Therefore I felt like I had superiors, most of whom were doctors, benevolent but possessing power. I had no rank, which is interesting considering the sort of military fantasy I had there.

The phenomenon that haunted me for quite a while, as I got in touch with my new surroundings at Communicare, was that I was back in the Navy. For several weeks I was haunted by the awareness that I had reported to a new base and was anticipating the opportunity of delivering speech to the parents of new Navy recruits. My speech was intended to put the parents at ease because they had assisted their children in making the good decision of choosing Navy.

I think I occasionally saluted my doctors in charge and complained to one that I was being given the runaround about making the speech.

One time I called my personal physician at home in upstate New York to complain to him. As it turned out, his wife reported to me that it was unfortunate and that she would tell her husband as soon as he got home. I am pleased to say that I never heard from him, so it goes to show you that even crazy you can sound convincing on flat ground on the phone.

But as luck would have it I was due for an appointment with a neurologist in Saratoga[6] soon thereafter. He asked me how were things going and how was I adapting. I said fine but launched into my Navy story and how frustrated I had become over not being able to give my speech to recruits' parents.

I noticed he was making notes as I rambled on. As our appointment seemed to be concluding he excused himself for a few minutes and when he came back his mood seemed a little brighter. He clasped me on the shoulder, the way docs sometime do, and dismissed me saying something like, "Well, I think you're making good progress, but I'd get rid of that Navy story." And showed me the way out. I assumed on his break he'd had enough time to call my base and talk to my "CO".

When I got back to Communicare the masquerade's final act included a note to 'whomever it concerns' to, "Please excuse patient Moffett from the need to make any speeches while he recovers." The note was handed to me by the doc who was my chief in charge.

To this day. I still remember aspects of my fantasy but I never repeated my "Navy story" again. And just for the record, I really was in the Navy and thought it a great branch of the service, sir (salute).

The Communicare facility was well tailored to not convey the impression to those who were housed there that they were incapacitated or mentally short of a full box. But there were some house rules and one was you could not walk off grounds without escort (evidently there had been some wanderers or walkers off).

In fact, I became one of the walkers, always wanting to go farther than was reasonably permitted.

In lieu of wandering off the property, I started walking or balancing on the wooden beams, actually railroad ties that bordered the flower beds

---

6 Bill refers to the facility in Saratoga. It was Sarasota.

marking the mowed lawn boundaries. One day I was seen by one of the staff docs doing my walking act and was criticized for showing off, or so my nurse walking buddy told me.

I lost those garden walking privileges. But in the resulting process, my balance had much improved and my stability was better, neither of which had been my goal. But I gave up garden "the walking" and very soon thereafter I was released to go home to Cape Coral.

I didn't have a point to make about tie walking except that it was mildly exhilarating, so let it go knowing that I had gained some strength nonetheless.

But in that same vein, I did broaden the independence and breadth of my walks, which was one of the first times I was aware of prolonged self-assertion following the accident. A good sign I think, in retrospect.

Prior to joining the patients at Communicare, cooking had been a minor passion and in fact I did most of the cooking in the house, both because I liked doing it and because my spouse was glad to be relieved of the necessity. By the time we had landed in Florida, most of our six kids had married and/or moved away and had various working responsibilities of their own but I was used to it and was still cooking in Florida when we reached Communicare.

As the goal of the institution was to get the various impaired under their care back to daily functioning, while making sure they were skillful and safe enough, at a point in my tutelage I was assigned someone to supervise my actions during a resumption of potentially dangerous tasks. So it became time for me to be observed cooking a simple meal under supervision.

When at home in upstate New York, Hope and I and the kids had created a cookbook of some of our favorites, so it was easy to come up with an idea. Soup would be my repertoire to be observed. Not just any soup, but our Italian favorite, minestrone[7]. I remember that I got everything rolling along pretty well but then reached a blank spot where my memory failed and had to find and ask Hope "What do I do next?"

Turned out she was as uncertain as I so I had to punt: I added a can of Progresso soup by same name, gave it a stir and, "Voila. Soups on."

It tasted pretty good and I think I got an A-Okay for the effort—for ingenuity if not culinary success, and having not set fire anything the hospital cared about, I was okayed to go to the next proving grounds. In

---

[7] *In his cooking event at Communicare, Bill remembers making minestrone soup. It was actually chili.*

this rehabilitation environment for brain-injured patients, no step is taken if not done successfully.

One of the low spots on the Communicare expedition was the communal food operation. The chow line was somewhat Navy in that there was usually a hot or warm entrée as one option and typically a second choice, a soup and sandwich-like thing. As food lines go, the food was good enough but the ambiance of the institutional space sucked. Get it down and get out, type of thing.

Also, the room wasn't packed with people you really wanted to dine with. Consequently, I looked for and really longed to ride with someone who could drive us to one of the good Florida seaside restaurants.

This was a double outing for me! One, I got "off base," two I got to dine with someone I loved or admired, and three, I got a very satisfactory change of food and lots of good cooking aromas to experience.

The ambiance was great, too, being on the ocean water with a refreshing wind and aroma of the sea. Being the chef in our family, I have a strong interest in food and cooking, so escaping the predictability of the food line was a very welcome change.

Though my brain injury prognosis called for no drinking, I was still a serious wino and occasionally cheated a little with a glass of wine with lunch—but don't tell!

Circumstances have combined since then and wine has been mostly off my diet and that has taken its toll on my cooking interest, sorry to say. But I still believe that wine and good food are a happy couple that I want around me as often as possible!

Packing to leave unexpectedly was one of the weird behavior features I adopted at Communicare after the brain injury. And it used to really piss off my wife, Hope.

Often before she arrived I would develop the illusion that I was leaving with her. So she would arrive and come to my room and might find my bags packed and neatly ordered outside my door.

She'd be pissed and say. "Why are your bags packed beside the door? You are not going anywhere!"

I'd give her a disappointed, "Oh shit, I thought we were going home today."

Next time she came, she'd be relieved to not find bags out by the front door, then do her own, "Oh shit!" when she'd come in and find my bags packed and lined up inside.

This happened too many times for the maintenance of polite behavior. I guess I really wanted to get out of there. She still had a two hour drive back to Cape Coral. So my being at Communicare was not fun for her either.

During my recovery I learned an interesting new expression.

I had been invited by a couple of my docs to take a walk down to the lunch room. Along the way, I frequently let my left shoulder collide with supporting pillars for the walkway roof.

No mention of this behavior was made during the walk, but shortly thereafter my doc's progress report remarked on "left side neglect." Maybe you have to be a professional neurologist to use this term.

When I asked about it, my doc said, "Remember those posts you walked into before lunch?"

Well, I thought, so what?

"We call that left side neglect—you were not aware you were doing it!"

I still didn't think it was strange.

I realize now that it could be a big deal if left uncorrected. So if you see a guy walking down the street bumping things with his left shoulder, be sure to say "Hi Bill!"

The clinical objective of brain injury recovery is to help the subject to regain strength and reconnect with elements of his previous life as soon as possible. For me, this involved working at a keyboard and putting thoughts on file or paper—what I had been doing several hours a day every day before the accident.

When I got at my first computer in rehab, it was a mess of hunt and peck. I was also trying out "brain games" on the keyboard to stimulate my brain in some way.

Sometimes the drill was just being left alone to find my way to the correct office on the campus.

But lest you think it was nothing but hard, painful work, some of it required sitting on the patio reading books in the sun. On occasions when my wife would come, she often found me working on my tan with a book. Good therapy!

But soon it would be time to sit back down at that computer and practice brain games. A site called "Luminosity" was one of my doc's favorites. There were never any standards one had to meet, but sometimes old ways and customs still ruled. You want to compete as you used to. Trouble was, I never played with a computer doing games—you are supposed to work at one! Consequently, I often found their rules and regulations too challenging.

Fortunately, as time went by, they became more interesting and easy. And this reminds me of a day when my wife arrived and found me not working computer drills. She asked, "Why not?"

I said that they were boring and not productive.

She gave me that eye only a wife can, saying, "But if you don't show them you can do the work, they may not let you leave!"

That was all it took to get me buckled down and back to work!

On a happy note, we have a large family of six kids, ten grandkids, and lots of brothers on Hope's side. I grieve that I cannot remember better that they were all there, along with some good friends from up north, vacationing then in Florida. I do remember being surrounded by loved ones and it was comforting that they often helped Hope through some of the rough spots, which were indeed plentiful for her. This was perhaps the best part of "My" story.

Addendum: About Brain Injury
Rancho Los Amigos Scale / The Levels of Coma
From: http://waiting.com/rancholosamigos.html

I. No Response
A person at this level will:
- not respond to sounds, sights, touch or movement.

II. Generalized Response
A person at this level will:
- begin to respond to sounds, sights, touch or movement;
- respond slowly, inconsistently, or after a delay;
- respond in the same way to what he hears, sees or feels. Responses may include chewing, sweating, breathing faster, moaning, moving and/or increasing blood pressure.

III. Localized Response
A person at this level will:
- be awake on and off during the day;
- make more movements than before;
- react more specifically to what he sees, hears or feels. For example, he may turn towards a sound, withdraw from pain, and attempt to watch a person move around the room;
- react slowly and inconsistently;
- begin to recognize family and friends;
- follow some simple directions such as "Look at me" or "squeeze my hand";
- begin to respond inconsistently to simple questions with "yes" or "no" head nods.

IV. Confused-Agitated
A person at this level will:
- be very confused and frightened;
- not understand what he feels, or what is happening around him;
- overreact to what he sees, hears or feels by hitting, screaming, using abusive language, or thrashing about. This is because of the confusion;

- be restrained so he doesn't hurt himself;
- be highly focused on his basic needs; i.e., eating, relieving pain, going back to bed, going to the bathroom, or going home;
- may not understand that people are trying to help him;
- not pay attention or be able to concentrate for a few seconds;
- have difficulty following directions;
- recognize family/friends some of the time;
- with help, be able to do simple routine activities such as feeding himself, dressing or talking.

V. Confused-Inappropriate, Non-Agitated
A person at this level will:
- be able to pay attention for only a few minutes;
- be confused and have difficulty making sense of things outside himself;
- not know the date, where he is or why he is in the hospital;
- not be able to start or complete everyday activities, such as brushing his teeth, even when physically able. He may need step-by-step instructions;
- become overloaded and restless when tired or when there are too many people around; have a very poor memory, he will remember past events from before the accident better than his daily routine or information he has been told since the injury;
- try to fill in gaps in memory by making things up; (confabulation)
- may get stuck on an idea or activity (perseveration) and need help switching to the next part of the activity;
- focus on basic needs such as eating, relieving pain, going back to bed, going to the bathroom, or going home.

VI. Confused-Appropriate

A person at this level will:

- be somewhat confused because of memory and thinking problems, he will remember the main points from a conversation, but forget and confuse the details. For example, he may remember he had visitors in the morning, but forget what they talked about;
- follow a schedule with some assistance, but becomes confused by changes in the routine;
- know the month and year, unless there is a serious memory problem;
- pay attention for about 30 minutes, but has trouble concentrating when it is noisy or when the activity involves many steps. For example, at an intersection, he may be unable to step off the curb, watch for cars, watch the traffic light, walk, and talk at the same time;
- brush his teeth, get dressed, feed himself etc., with help;
- know when he needs to use the bathroom;
- do or say things too fast, without thinking first;
- know that he is hospitalized because of an injury, but will not understand all the problems he is having;
- be more aware of physical problems than thinking problems;
- associate his problems with being in the hospital and think he will be fine as soon as he goes home.

VII. Automatic-Appropriate

A person at this level will:

- follow a set schedule;
- be able to do routine self-care without help, if physically able. For example, he can dress or feed himself independently; have problems in new situations and may become frustrated or act without thinking first;
- have problems planning, starting, and following through with activities;
- have trouble paying attention in distracting or stressful situations. For example, family gatherings, work, school, church, or sports events;

- not realize how his thinking and memory problems may affect future plans and goals. Therefore, he may expect to return to his previous lifestyle or work;
- continue to need supervision because of decreased safety awareness and judgement. He still does not fully understand the impact of his physical or thinking problems;
- think slower in stressful situations;
- be inflexible or rigid, and he may be stubborn. However, his behaviors are related to his brain injury;
- be able to talk about doing something, but will have problems actually doing it.

VIII. Purposeful-Appropriate
A person at this level will:
- realize that he has a problem in his thinking and memory;
- begin to compensate for his problems;
- be more flexible and less rigid in his thinking. For example, he may be able to come up with several solutions to a problem;
- be ready for driving or job training evaluation;
- be able to learn new things at a slower rate;
- still become overloaded with difficult, stressful or emergency situations;
- show poor judgement in new situations and may require assistance;
- need some guidance making decisions;
- have thinking problems that may not be noticeable to people who did not know the person before the injury.

Addendum: Family

To help readers keep straight all of our kids, here is a list:

Bill's biological children are:

- Andra, married to Marijn Dekkers, with three daughters, Alexandra, Stephanie, Marina, moved from Boston to Germany in 2009.
- Tim Moffett, married to Wendy, with two children, Samantha and Jacob, living in Victor, New York, only half an hour away from Ferris Hills.
- Allison, married to John Santos, with two sons, Gabriel and Jude, living in Hector, New York, about an hour or so away.

Hope's biological children are:

- Kathy, married to Matt Licata, with son Matthew, also living in Victor, New York.
- Mark Merletti unmarried, living in Corning, New York, an hour and a half away.
- Rob Merletti divorced from Jennifer, with two daughters, Milan and Lucca, living in California.

Addendum: In a Nutshell

Here, in a nutshell, is what I learned through our ordeal.

If you have been in an accident, whether you are the driver, passenger in the car hit, or in the car that hits another, find a qualified lawyer. I hate all of those commercials by "injury" attorneys, but hiring an attorney made the care Bill received possible. Bill Partridge, our lawyer, uncovered funds we would have not understood were there.

- After our experience I am more convinced than ever that a patient needs an advocate. This is especially true of one who is not awake. Caretakers try to do their best, but human error is always possible, and any one such error can be fatal. Appeal to relatives, friends, hire private duty nurses. While the patient cannot speak for himself, have someone with him 24/7.

- Especially with brain injuries, take nothing the patient says personally. This is hard to do when dealing with a loved one. As Doctor Galloway pointed out many families can't take the abuse heaped on them by a brain-injured patient. Bill was often verbally abusive and at the time it was painful. In retrospect, I wish I could have stayed more detached.

- Many brain-injured patients think they are ready to go home far earlier than they are. We heard of cases where patients who had looked normal were allowed to go home. But when they discovered that they could not master routines that had been easy for them prior to their injury, they often became depressed. Many turned to alcohol and drugs.

- Ask others to pray for your loved one, or to send positive thoughts. We were not churchgoers prior to this accident, but hometown churches placed us on their prayer list. We both felt this warmth almost physically, and today think this outpouring of love and positive thinking played a role in Bill's recovery.

- Investigate CaringBridge. It allows the caretaker to post one message that goes out to many people. Staying in touch with all relatives and friends individually quickly becomes exhausting. Caring-Bridge is a lifesaver.

- Take some time off. The caretaker sometimes becomes so immersed in the role she thinks no one else can take care of a loved one. When one of your family members or friends offers to take over for you, unless you have grave doubt about their ability to oversee your loved one, take the time off! You will become depleted otherwise. For a caretaker, brain injury recovery is a long haul, and the days and nights are exhausting. Time away allows the caretaker to rest and come back to the role with a new perspective.

- Take Peter Hansberger's advice. If what happens in your loved one's care will affect him or her a year down the road, speak up. If it won't be remembered, and isn't harmful, let it go. Being a caretaker can arouse all of one's protective (maternal) feelings, and it is tempting to try to protect your loved one from everything. This is neither wise nor possible.

- Let yourself cry. If it weren't for the nights in the hotel when I let it all rip, I think I would have lost my mind. Always after a good cry and a glass of wine, a modicum of peace would return. The lump in my throat that seemed always there would disappear for a while.

- Don't expect life to go back to normal. After a severe brain injury it seldom does. Try to remember that your life hasn't been taken from you but it has changed. You will have challenges and trials you can meet more successfully if you aren't aiming for exactly what was.

Acknowledgements

As I look back at the experiences of the last seven plus years, one thing I know for sure. There is no way we could have survived without the support of so many.

It is always gratifying to observe your own children behaving with strength, love and dignity. Our children did that and more. They came from far away, often at considerable sacrifice, leaving behind spouses, children, and careers, taking vacation time to hold us up, especially during the terrible early days. Later, we spent many hours talking on the phone or e-mailing as we faced the decisions that had to be made to move Bill's care ahead.

What would we have done without my brothers? I would have given up several times if I had not been shored-up by the strength, love and kindness of my brothers and sisters-in-law. The Guzzettas never left me alone. One of them was always with me. John, my oldest brother, and Fran Chapman, his wife, came to spend nights with me when I was at home in Cape Coral, even though John was in a neck brace and would have been much more comfortable in his own bed. Chas, my second brother in age, came multiple times, especially during crucial events, helping me make decisions, and giving me his arm to lean on. My youngest brother, Art, and his wife Diana gave up their first year of retirement to be there for us whenever and however we needed them. It is not possible to express enough gratitude for such sacrifices.

We are blessed with good friends. They arranged for Bill to have at least one familiar face every day during the times I needed to be away from him, helped us find rehab facilities, came to us wherever we were to keep our spirits up. John and Jeanne Kremer, Peter and Joette Knott, Raelene Shippee-Rice, Peter and Eileen Honsberger and Don and Nonie White (who could not travel to be with us, but stayed close to their phone at all times). All gave of themselves with their unique abilities. For any friends I have left out, please feel my love and gratitude.

I must acknowledge the skills of the caretakers, their caring, and their willingness to immerse themselves in Bill's recovery. So much has changed in the treatment of brain injury in just the last decade that caretakers must study and continue to improve their skill sets. Deepest appreciation.

201

A special thank you to The Reverend Richard McCaughey and Jennifer Klein who through their eight week course, Healing Pathways, continue to give hope and purpose to countless numbers of people in this community. Both expert presenters and counselors, the many hours they spend is volunteer time. Participating in Healing Pathways through two series helped me sort through many emotions, and gave me the ability to deal with the dilemmas we faced throughout the years of Bill's recuperation and other family crises.

The Canandaigua Writers Group (CWG). This is a gathering of fine people, bound by their love of writing. They never fail to be supportive and encouraging of one another. Meeting with this group once a month always moved me ahead in my writing and helped me believe in myself as a writer. I feel I would not have produced this book without their support, and I am deeply grateful to each and every one.

Three members of the CWG I am especially grateful to: Sally Crozier, who was the first editor of this manuscript, the talented Karen Sorce, who spent many hours working on a design for the cover, and Deb Massey not only my editor, but my hand holder and cheerleader. The generosity and creativity of these talented women added immeasurably to the finished product of this book. Thank you, friends.

ABOUT THE AUTHOR

Hope Moffett lives in the lovely Finger Lakes village of Canandaigua, NY with her husband, Bill.

Hope and Bill published Vineyard & Winery Management, a trade magazine for the wine and grape industry in the United States and Canada, for 35 years. The publication also sponsored national trade shows and wine judgings. The couple were themselves accomplished wine judges, and participated in many wine judging events all over the country.

They are very proud of their a blended family of six grown children, their spouses and ten grandchildren.

They had retired only months before their tragic automobile accident.